When Anger Hurts Your Kids

A PARENT'S GUIDE

McKay
·
Fanning
·
Paleg
·
Landis

NEW HARBINGER PUBLICATIONS, INC.

Publisher's Note

This publication is designed to provide accurate and authoritative information in regard to the subject matter covered. It is sold with the understanding that the publisher is not engaged in rendering psychological, financial, legal, or other professional services. If expert assistance or counseling is needed, the services of a competent professional should be sought.

Distributed in the U.S.A. by Publishers Group West; in Canada by Raincoast Books; in Great Britain by Hi Marketing, Ltd.; in South Africa by Real Books, Ltd.; in Australia by Boobook; and in New Zealand by Tandem Press.

Copyright © 1996 by   Matthew McKay, Ph.D., Paatrick Fanning
New Harbinger Publications, Inc.
5674 Shattuck Avenue
Oakland, CA 94609

Cover design by SHELBY DESIGNS & ILLUSTRATES
Text design by Tracy Marie Powell

Library of Congress Catalog Card Number: 95-72228
ISBN 1-57224-045-8 Paperback

Printed in the United States

New Harbinger Publications' Web site address: www.newharbinger.com

05   04   03

15   14   13   12   11   10   9

For all the children

"A great man is one who knows that he was not put on earth to be part of a process through which a child can be hurt."
—Murray Kempton

Contents

We wish to express our grateful appreciation to Joan Lidsker, Ph.D., who conducted many of the in-depth interviews in our pilot study; to Jude McKay, R.N., Karen Halliburton, and Christian Halliburton who analyzed the data from the interview transcripts; to Juergen Korbanka, Ph.D., and Michele Waters for their invaluable help with the statistical analysis of our survey data; to Adah Maurer, Ph.D., executive director of End Violence Against the Next Generation, for her advice on current research regarding the effects of corporal punishment; to Leslie Tilley for her fine work as editor; and to our colleagues at Publishers Group West for their enthusiastic interest in this book.

1

The Effects of Parental Anger

Have you ever

Become really angry at your child?

Yelled or slapped your child or lost control?

Felt discouraged and guilty later?

Resolved to stay calm?

But kept getting angry anyway?

If so, this book is for you.

When Anger Hurts Your Child is the result of a two-year study of 285 parents—normal, regular parents much like you, with normal, regular, infuriating kids much like yours. These parents completed a detailed survey, the results of which describe when and how parents get angry at their kids, the most important causes of anger, and the best ways to cope with anger.

We have put our study results together with other psychologists' research to show you how to create what we call a Master Plan for Anger Control. You can actually change what you think, what you do, and what you say, so that you can get the peace, quiet, love, and cooperation you want, without the anger.

The book is laid out step by step. In this chapter you'll find out about the effects of parental anger in general and why anger control is so important. In chapter 2 you'll look at your own family to see if you have a problem with anger. In chapter 3 you'll study what goes on in your mind and body when you get angry. Chapter 4 describes why kids act the way they do at different stages of development. In chapter 5 you'll begin to learn to control your anger, starting with changing what you think. Chapter 6 is about changing what you do, and chapter 7 covers changing what you say to your children. In chapter 8 you will put it all together in your Master Plan for Anger Control.

All Parents Get Angry

Parenting is a hard job. It would be tough if it were your *only* job. But every parent has so many competing responsibilities. It's no surprise, given the demands pulling you from every direction, that you feel stressed and angry some of the time.

Studies show that anger is a concern for a large percentage of parents. Over half the parents in one survey (Frude and Goss 1979) said they had lost their temper and hit their child "really hard." Another 40 percent feared that they might lose their temper and really hurt their child in the future. In our study, two-thirds of the parents reported feeling anger to the point of shouting or screaming at their children an average of five times per week. These were normal parents with normal children, but the majority had an intense anger episode nearly every day. These frequency rates are disturbing enough, but a study by Juergen Korbanka and Matthew McKay (1995) found that, overall, emotional support diminishes as parental yelling, threatening, and hitting increases. In other words, kids get less of every kind of nurturing and encouragement as parents get more angry.

Anger Leads to More Corporal Punishment

The 1985 National Family Violence Survey found that 90 percent of parents in the United States use corporal punishment by the time a child is two years old. If this seems young, consider that in 1965 one-fourth of U.S. infants one to six months old were spanked, and by twelve months nearly one-half were being physically punished (Straus 1994).

Since corporal punishment is almost a universal phenomenon, the most important issue becomes *how often* children are hit or spanked. The National Longitudinal Study of Youth discovered that in the United States, two-thirds of mothers with children under six said that they found it necessary to use corporal punishment three times per week—meaning that a large majority of mothers slap or hit their children an average of 150 times per year (Straus 1994). This statistic doesn't include the number of times children are also hit by fathers.

Frequency and intensity of parental anger is strongly related to the use of physical punishment. One recent study concluded that parents who yell often are the ones most likely to hit often (Hemenway, Solnick, and Carter 1994). And Carol Heussen (1986) found, in an important Canadian study, that parents are twice as likely to use physical punishment when they experience high levels of anger. A strong relationship also exists between physical abuse and blaming, name calling, and belittling. Korbanka and McKay (1995) found that parents who frequently engage in verbal attacks are more likely to cross over into physical attacks.

Corporal Punishment and Abuse

Because Americans use corporal punishment frequently, and because they resort to it most often in anger, there may be a relationship between hitting and the current epidemic of physical abuse. In his book, *Beating the Devil Out of Them: Corporal Punishment in American Families* (1994), sociologist Murray Straus reached this conclusion: "Scientific evidence showing that corporal punishment is a risk factor for abuse is as good or better than the evidence for other suspected causes. . . . The more corporal punishment is used, the greater the risk of escalation because corporal punishment does not help a child develop an internalized conscience. [Instead it] leads to more physically aggressive behavior by the child. The more parents rely on hitting, the more they will have to do it over time."

If anger-driven corporal punishment *is* a risk factor in abuse, America's children are paying a high price for our inability to find better ways to discipline. Child battery is now a leading cause of death for U.S. children, and twelve kids each day suffer brain damage from abuse. A 1994 national Gallop poll found that nearly one in twenty parents disciplined their children to a point where they were committing physical abuse. In the same year there were three million reported cases of physical abuse in the United States (*San Francisco Examiner*, December 7, 1995). Many of these children experienced serious physical injury, psychological trauma, or losses in intellectual or behavioral functioning as a consequence.

We have a national problem with anger at children. It's so serious that we are literally destroying—emotionally, mentally, and physically—vast numbers of the next generation.

Effects of Anger on Child Development

Social scientists have been investigating how parental anger and significant amounts of physical punishment affect a developing child. Here's what we currently know from research.

Children of Angry Parents Are More Aggressive and Noncompliant

Contrary to the popular wisdom of "spare the rod and spoil the child," angry punishments seem to create rebellious, uncontrolled children. A study of mothers' disciplinary techniques by Susan Crockenberg (1987) revealed that angry and punitive mothers had children who were themselves angry. Most significantly, these kids were also resistant and *noncompliant* compared with children of less angry mothers. This finding was confirmed by Zvi Strassberg, et al. (1994), who observed nearly 300 kindergarten children in the classroom and on the playground. Strassberg questioned these children's parents about how they had disciplined their kids during the past year. Children who had been spanked were found to be more aggressive toward other children. Strassberg concluded that it was the spanking itself, not its frequency, that triggered aggression, because spanking teaches kids that they can control others using physical coercion.

Penelope Trickett and Leon Kuczynski (1986) looked at the same issues with abused children. They found that children who have been abused either emotionally or physically commit "more aggressive transgressions" and are more likely to be oppositional than children of less angry parents.

Children of Angry Parents Are Less Empathic

Crockenberg (1987) found that children of angry mothers tend to distance themselves from that parent. It's quite possible that the mother-child bond is weakened by repeated punitive interactions. Researchers who study attachment have learned that the children who experience a breakdown in the empathic mother-child bond—for example, when the child's pain often goes unnoticed by the mother—are more self-focused. They have a hard time responding to anyone else's needs or pain.

Losing awareness of others was clearly demonstrated in Crockenberg's (1985) study of toddlers. She observed that more frequent maternal anger was associated with more frequent nonempathic reactions when toddlers were bystanders to someone else's distress.

Children of Angry Parents Have Poor Overall Adjustment

An important study by Abraham Tesser, et al. (1989) looked at the relationship between angry parent-child disagreements and adolescent adjustment. They kept track of disagreements about 44 specific issues, such as TV use and homework, and had mothers, fathers, and adolescents rate the degree of anger on each occasion.

They then measured the children's adjustment including assessments of academic competence, social competence, acting out, depression, and grade-point average, along with other data. The level of adjustment in *every one* of these areas was negatively related to the number of angry parent-child discussions. And just as significant, adjustment in each area was *positively* related to the number of calm discussions.

The research evidence clearly indicates that the amount of anger expressed in the family will affect your child's performance in nearly every important area of his or her adolescent life. Anger casts a long shadow, blighting not just the moment, but the emotional, academic, and social functioning of your child.

Parental Anger and Delinquency

Since young children react to chronic parental anger with rebelliousness and anger of their own, it's not surprising that there's a relationship between parental anger and adolescent delinquency. Straus (1994) found that the more corporal punishment parents use, the more their adolescent children are likely to show delinquent patterns. In Straus' study, only 5 percent of teens whose parents used no corporal punishment developed delinquent behavior. On the other hand, adolescents whose parents used corporal punishment more than thirty times a year had a 25 percent delinquency rate.

Phillip Grevin, in his book *Spare the Child* (1990), concluded that "the overwhelming evidence now available on the roots of delinquency and crime suggest that corporal punishment is a major factor in generating the rage, aggression, and impulses for revenge that fuel the emotions, fantasies, and actions of individuals who become delinquents or criminals." There is currently a great deal of concern about the violence of our society. If Grevin is right, we should worry less about how the media displays mayhem and more about how anger and physical punishment at home can plant in our children the seeds of antisocial rage. It takes a long time for these seeds to sprout and grow, but it is increasingly clear that repeated episodes of parental anger only serve to irrigate our country's crop of batterers and violent criminals.

Recent evidence is also mounting that the effects of anger pass on from generation to generation. Lisa Zaidi, John Knutson, and John Mehm (1989) found that parents who had themselves grown up in punitive families were more likely to have children displaying antisocial and aggressive problems. And many other studies verify that approximately a third of abused children go on to abuse their own kids (Oliver 1993).

Effects of Parental Anger on the Adult Child

Children of angry parents grow up to face more severe problems than those who are raised in less angry homes. Women, in particular, seem to bear the scars of early exposure to anger. Korbanka and McKay (1995) examined family histories of 200 subjects (men and women) and determined whether their parents used threatening or nonthreatening discipline styles. A threatening style involves more frequent hitting, yelling, and scaring with threats of dire consequences. Women who grew up in families using a threatening style experienced more emotional numbness, as well as a painful yearning for closeness and intimacy. They also had shorter, less stable friendships. The men in the study suffered none of these problems. But they appeared to have more difficulty sustaining *romantic* attachments, with their relationships lasting six months less on average than those of men who grew up in nonthreatening families.

Depression

Depression in adults has many causes. One contributing factor appears to be the amount of corporal punishment experienced in childhood. Straus (1994) reports that adults whose parents hit them as adolescents have higher rates of depression than those whose parents disciplined them in other ways. People who were physically punished as adolescents are also more likely to have thoughts about suicide. This is more disturbing evidence that parental anger, physically expressed, seems to affect how children feel about themselves and the world. Children who have been punished physically grow up to be less accepting of who they are and less confident that they can achieve what they need to be happy. Because parental anger so often conveys the message "you are bad," it may be that children simply absorb that picture of themselves until it forms a cornerstone of their identity. Then, as adults, they expect very little of the world—because they believe they don't deserve to have love, success, or happiness.

Related to depression and lowered self-esteem is the prevalence of eating disorders among women who come from angry families. The more parents hit, yell, and threaten, the more likely their adult daughters will struggle with compulsive eating (Korbanka and McKay 1995). For many people, bingeing is an effort to mask or numb feelings of worthlessness. The old "you are bad" message sent by angry parents must constantly be "stuffed away" with food.

Alienation

Alienation is described by Straus (1994) as a combination of two strong feelings. The first component is a sense of *powerlessness*—the conviction that you have little control over your life and few resources to meet important needs. The second component of alienation is a "who cares" feeling, characterized by an absence of firm moral standards and the tendency to do whatever is expedient to get by.

Straus found that adolescents who experienced more frequent corporal punishment develop a greater sense of alienation as adults. His conclusion is supported by the established link between depression and physical punishment. Depression has been described as *learned helplessness*—the realization that no matter what you do, there's little chance that you can change or control your environment. The learned helplessness of depression closely resembles the powerless feelings at the core of alienation.

There's an important reason for the "who cares" absence of standards in physically punished adolescents. Children who are physically punished have less opportunity to develop an internalized conscience. When a parent threatens and scares a child into compliance, the only learning that takes place is "Don't, or you'll get hit." So kids get sneaky, trying to figure out what they can get away with. Anything is OK as long as Mom or Dad isn't watching or likely to find out.

The reason corporal punishment stunts the growth of conscience is that your child no longer tries to please you and make you proud. Instead, he or she is only trying to avoid pain. It's the desire for their parents' acceptance and approval that helps children "internalize" the rules and make them their own.

Spouse Abuse

We've already explored how anger can be passed from parent to child, like a dark inheritance. But it can also touch the partners of those who've grown up in an angry family. Men who experienced significant corporal punishment as adolescents are more likely to hit their spouses (Straus 1994). Again, this makes sense because corporal punishment teaches that problems can be solved by hitting. The lesson is, "If you don't like how someone acts, if they seem disrespectful, slap them." The inevitable struggles that occur in any intimate relationship can trigger violent solutions from men who saw a parent resolving conflict through acts of force and intimidation.

Career and Economic Achievement

The emotional consequences of punitive parenting—numbness, depression, alienation, and anger—may limit achievement levels later in life. Even among people who complete college, the more corporal punishment they experienced during adolescence, the less likely they are to reach the highest levels of occupational and economic success (Straus 1994).

Parents want their children to have every opportunity to reach full potential. Yet, an angry discipline style may be undermining the parent's otherwise strong efforts to help a child become everything he or she can be.

How This Book Can Help

Nothing is carved in stone about how you have to be with your children. Things can change. If you are concerned about your anger and the ways it affects your kids, this book can be a tool to make real and enduring changes in how you handle parent-child conflict.

You can learn to recognize and cope with early warning signs of stress *before* anger erupts. You can learn to recognize and change the "trigger thoughts" that ignite your anger. You can learn to identify and respond to the *real* causes of your child's misbehavior. You can learn problem-solving techniques that short circuit the old anger cycles. And you can develop a master plan for controlling your anger, which can profoundly change your relationship with your child.

These are not idle promises. The things you'll learn in this book have demonstrated effectiveness for parents who use them. But that's the key: You have to *use* them. It's not enough to read this book and passively absorb ideas. You'll have to *work* at developing new skills—doing the exercises, practicing new ways of talking and responding to your kids, learning stress-reduction and other coping strategies. But if you do the work, your old patterns of anger and frustration with your children will diminish. You'll feel more effective as a parent. And your kids will grow up free of anger's damaging effects.

2

Do You Have a Problem?

Her screeching and crying were driving me crazy—to the point where I thought I might hit her if it didn't stop. I yelled at her and was rough with her when I put her in her room. I probably spent the next hour sitting on the couch thinking "I can't believe this is me, totally out of control, screaming at my kid like this." The fact is, I don't even recognize myself when I get that angry. And it scares me.

—Father of a five-year-old.

As a parent, you probably know all too well that these feelings are not unusual. In fact, experiences such as feeling out of control, having a momentary impulse to hit or strike out at your child, or feeling remorseful after a confrontation with your child are more likely to occur than not. Being a parent is probably the most stressful job you'll ever take on. Late nights, long hours, an infinite list of responsibilities, and constant demands for your attention are all part of the territory. Every parent feels the effects of these conditions, and every parent struggles at times with overwhelming stress and sudden, lashing anger.

If you are reading this book, you have some concern about your anger as a parent. But how big a problem is it? Researcher Carol Heusson (1986) found that a majority of parents have experienced feeling so angry at their child that they feared losing control. So at what point is anger considered problematic? The main focus of this chapter is to help you identify whether you have a problem with anger. The chapter will outline three steps you can take to assess your anger level and identify the effects it is having on your relationship with your child. As you move through the assessment process, try to look back at your experiences with parental anger as honestly as possible. Also try to be compassionate toward yourself and your child as you review old episodes. Remember, *all* parents struggle at times with anger.

Assessing Your Anger Level

The difficulty with assessing your own anger level is that anger, like all other emotions, is a subjective experience. One parent may assume that a daily blowup with her eight-year-old child is perfectly normal, if not inevitable, and doesn't indicate a problem. Another parent may feel wracked with guilt for yelling at his five-year-old child twice in one week. As there are no obvious guidelines or standards for parents to measure themselves against, it can be very difficult to get a sense of whether your level of anger is particularly high or low or about average.

One way to get an objective idea of your overall anger level is to compare yourself directly to other parents. Virginia DeRoma at the VA Medical Center in Biloxi, Mississippi, and David Hansen (1994) at the University of Nebraska at Lincoln developed the Parental Anger Inventory (PAI) for just such a purpose. By looking at the scores of 166 parents, they were able to determine an average range, as well as which scores indicated problematic anger levels. The following is a copy of the PAI questionnaire used in their research. Take a few moments right now to complete this inventory.

Parental Anger Inventory *

Below is a list of situations that often make parents angry. After reading the description of a situation, please rate the situation in two ways:

1. Tell *how* angry the situation makes you.

2. Tell whether or not the situation *is a problem* for you right now (or has been in the past month).

Rate with this scale how angry each situation makes you:
1 = not at all, 2 = a little bit, 3 = somewhat, 4 = quite a bit, 5 = extremely. Place this number in the space on the left.

If the situation has been a problem for you in the last month, mark it with an X in the problem column at the right of the page.

Be sure to rate your anger response to each situation—even if you don't mark it as a problem in the past month.

For each of the following problem situations, please complete all of column 1 ("How Angry?") first, and *then* rate column 2 ("Problem?").

*How angry does this
situation make you?*
1 – 2 – 3 – 4 – 5
not at all   extremely

*Check here if this
situation has been
a problem in the
last month?*

_____ 1. Your child gets out of bed after being put in bed.   _____

_____ 2. You ask your child to do something and he or   _____
         she won't do it.

_____ 3. Your child complains (for example, because he   _____
         or she has to turn off the TV or stop doing
         something fun).

* Reproduced with permission of the authors.

*How angry does this
situation make you?
1 – 2 – 3 – 4 – 5
not at all   extremely*

*Check here if this
situation has been
a problem in the
last month?*

____   4. Your child makes messes around the house.   ____

____   5. Your child wastes things around the house
(like toothpaste or food).   ____

____   6. Your child does something that bothers you
over and over again (like playing a record or
singing a nursery rhyme or song).   ____

____   7. Your child does something (plays with
something of yours or goes outside) without
asking permission.   ____

____   8. You tell your child to do something and he or
she says "I already did" when you know this is
not true.   ____

____   9. Your child gets into something he or she is not
allowed to (like makeup or tools).   ____

____   10. Your child does not make his or her bed in the
morning.   ____

____   11. Your child leaves his or her things laying
around the house.   ____

____   12. Your child does something you asked him or
her not to do.   ____

____   13. Your child screams and yells when you say
"no" after he or she asks for something in a
store or at home.   ____

____   14. Your child screams and yells at his or her sisters
and/or brothers.   ____

____   15. Your child makes too much noise when you are
busy working or talking.   ____

How angry does this
situation make you?
1 – 2 – 3 – 4 – 5
not at all   extremely

Check here if this
situation has been
a problem in the
last month?

_____ 16. Your child bothers you when you are busy working or talking.   _____

_____ 17. Your child gets into things he or she shouldn't when you are at someone else's house.   _____

_____ 18. Your child breaks things on purpose.   _____

_____ 19. Your child doesn't listen to you in public.   _____

_____ 20. Your child uses curse words when he or she talks to you.   _____

_____ 21. Your child spills food or a drink.   _____

_____ 22. Your child pouts or puts on a long face because he or she can't have his or her way.   _____

_____ 23. Your child says things that are not true on purpose.   _____

_____ 24. Your child refuses to go to bed.   _____

_____ 25. Your child plays too loudly.   _____

_____ 26. Your child wets the bed.   _____

_____ 27. Your child has a bowel movement in his or her pants.   _____

_____ 28. Your child takes things that don't belong to him or her.   _____

_____ 29. Your child won't answer you when you ask him or her a question.   _____

_____ 30. Your child can't sit still.   _____

_____ 31. Your child demands something immediately.   _____

*How angry does this
situation make you?
1 – 2 – 3 – 4 – 5
not at all   extremely*

*Check here if this
situation has been
a problem in the
last month?*

_____ 32. Your child pretends not to hear when you   _____
speak.

_____ 33. Your child does not share toys.   _____

_____ 34. Your child interrupts you when you are talking _____
with someone.

_____ 35. Your child constantly picks up things when you _____
are in a store.

_____ 36. Your child constantly touches things when you   _____
are in a store.

_____ 37. Your child won't stay in his or her seat during _____
car trips.

_____ 38. Your child's teacher calls on the phone to tell _____
you about a school problem.

_____ 39. Your child screams, yells, and/or gets in fights _____
during car trips.

_____ 40. Your child does poorly in school.   _____

_____ 41. Your child cries (for a reason other than being _____
physically hurt).

_____ 42. Your child throws food at the table.   _____

_____ 43. Your child repeatedly gets up and down from   _____
the dinner table before he or she is finished
eating.

_____ 44. Your child doesn't do his or her chores.   _____

_____ 45. Your child misbehaves after you have had a   _____
bad day.

*How angry does this
situation make you?*
1 – 2 – 3 – 4 – 5
not at all   extremely

*Check here if this
situation has been
a problem in the
last month?*

_____ 46. Your child wanders away from home without   _____
          telling you.

_____ 47. Your child does not come right home from   _____
          school.

_____ 48. Your child touches or plays with something   _____
          dangerous.

_____ 49. Your child runs into the street.   _____

_____ 50. Your child climbs on counters or other   _____
          dangerous places around the house.

Now go back and add up all the numbers in the left-hand column of the PAI. The total of those numbers is your overall parental anger score. Out of the 166 parents who were surveyed by DeRoma and Hansen, the average score was 98. This means that 50 percent of the parents tested had a score of 98 points or less. Next add up the number of times you marked an X in the right-hand column of the inventory. In our own survey, the average number of times parents identified an item as problematic was 20. This means that 50 percent of the parents marked 20 or less of the items. Comparing your scores with these averages can give you a sense of where you are in relation to other parents.

Understanding the Results of the PAI

If you find that your overall anger score is more than 98, on this scale your anger levels are higher than average. You may have a problem with anger. However, at this point, it's important to recognize that the Parental Anger Inventory only tests one aspect of your anger experience. While this scale cannot reflect the quality of your parenting nor your abilities to cope with anger, it can tell you that you experience more anger than the average parent. As you move through the how-to chapters of this book, you can use the information you learned from the PAI to encourage you to set goals, and develop a program for change.

If you found that your anger level is average or below average for most parents, good. What this means is that your overall anger response is not unusually high. Nonetheless, it is still important to recognize that the PAI is limited in its scope. It reflects general trends among large groups of parents. While it can be very helpful in understanding how your experience compares with the norm, it does not reflect the unique characteristics of individual parent-child relationships. The effects of anger on your children may be problematic in ways that are not identified by the PAI.

Other Factors to Consider

Just as parents vary in their levels of anger, their tolerance for disappointment or frustration, and their abilities to cope with anger, children vary in their reaction to parental anger. As you evaluate the effects of anger on your parent-child relationship, one of the most important characteristics to consider is your child's *sensitivity* to anger. The same action that causes one child to storm off, only to forget about it an hour later, may leave another child in the grips of shame or resentment for the rest of the day. Children vary tremendously in their reaction to shouting, parental withdrawal, punishment, disapproval, and so on. While your anger level may be below average, your child's sensitivity to anger may be above average. To really understand whether anger is problematic in your relationship, it will help to look carefully at the unique characteristics of your child.

Another important characteristic to consider is your *style* of anger. The way parents cope with and express anger has a big influence on their children. A slightly annoyed parent who says to a child "I'm sick of hearing your voice—take your sissy whining someplace else" has probably done more damage than a really furious parent who says "I'm very, very angry about how all this turned out. I want you to go to your room and stay there until I call you." Even mild parental anger that is expressed as an attack on the identity of the child ("You're bad, stupid, just like your damn father.") or is expressed in the form of a threat ("Say that again and see what happens.") can have far more negative effects than extreme parental anger that is expressed appropriately ("Your screaming is making it impossible for me to be around you. Stay in your room until you are ready to have a real conversation."). Look closely at your style of anger and how that might be affecting the way your child experiences conflicts.

Assessing the Effect on Your Child

Looking for Danger Signs

It's important to remember that the same situation can affect you and your child in very different ways. What is experienced by you as a short spat might have a far larger impact on your child than you're aware of. Because children often can't communicate their feelings verbally, one of the most effective ways to learn about your child's experience is to watch his or her behavior. The following is a list of behaviors that are commonly seen in children who are being negatively affected by parental anger. Watch for these behaviors; they can be viewed as red flags that may indicate a problem.

- Your child is afraid to try things. His or her sensitivity to criticism prevents him from taking on challenges or tasks.

- Your child is overly abusive with a younger sibling or flies into angry rages in which he or she tries to hurt a younger child or sibling.

- Your child seems depressed or lethargic or lacks interest in age-appropriate activities.

- Your child resists spending time with you, going places with you, or sharing activities with you.

- Your child has behavior problems in school (is very withdrawn or temperamental and aggressive with other kids).

- Your child displays low self-esteem (puts people down, is constantly dissatisfied with his or her performance or be-

havior, or demonstrates a generally negative perception of
him- or herself).

- Your child appears to have little empathy when relating to
  people who are hurt or sad.

While the above list of red-flag behaviors is commonly associated with children who experience high levels of parental anger,
they may also be symptoms of other problems not related to anger
at all. Watching your child's behavior can't give you all the answers, but it can give you more data to consider as you build a
fuller picture of the complex dynamic that exists between you.

Talking to Your Child

Perhaps the best way to assess the effects of anger in your
parent-child relationship is to ask direct questions of your child.
This method is limited to children who are older and both able and
willing to express their feelings. If your child is old enough to talk
about his or her experiences but is uncomfortable sharing them
with you, you might consider enlisting the help of a third party,
such as a therapist or another adult whom the child trusts, so your
child has enough support to open up.

The following is a list of sample questions that you might use
in discussing the issue of parental anger with your child:

- Is it scary for you when I get angry?

- Do you feel bad about yourself when I'm angry with you?

- Does your bad feeling last a long time?

- Do you worry a lot that I'll get angry with you?

- Do you wonder when I'll get angry?

- Do you know the things that get me angry, or is it usually
  a surprise, where you never know what will upset me?

- When I get angry at you, do you feel scared that I'm going
  to hurt you?

You might add your own questions about specific issues that have worried you or made you suspect that your child is struggling or frightened with the way things are.

When Wanda asked her seven-year-old, Frank, some of these questions, she was surprised at his clear answers: "Yeah, I get scared when you hold my arm hard and talk loud. . . . Sometimes I feel bad at school when you get mad at me in the morning. . . . I think I'm bad. . . . I never know what makes you mad—you can laugh when I don't like breakfast or get mad about it." Frank took Wanda's questions quite seriously. And Wanda did the same with Frank's answers.

Keeping an Anger Diary

So far the focus of this chapter has been on assessing your anger level and investigating the effects of parental anger on both you and your child. Now it's time to learn more about actual conflict situations—what happens that gets you mad, how much anger you feel and express, and how things resolve. To do this, you need to keep an anger diary. As you focus your attention on the causes and effects of anger on your daily life, patterns will begin to emerge that will help you understand the complex anger dynamic that exists between you and your child. In later chapters of the book, the diary will help you make important changes in your thoughts and behavior during conflicts with your child.

The first step is to buy a notebook or a looseleaf binder and paper. Keep it in your bedroom or study or anyplace where you have time to yourself. Starting today, and during the entire time you are working through this book, record each anger episode with your child in the diary. Start your anger diary by defining five columns, under which you will record the following:

- The date.

- The situation that incited your anger.

- How much anger you felt, on a scale of 1 to 10, where 1 is a very mild feeling of anger and 10 is the most angry you have ever felt.

- How much anger you expressed, on a scale of 1 to 10, where 1 is a very mild expression (like mentioning calmly that you felt angry), and 10 is the most extreme expression of anger you have ever displayed.

- The outcome of the situation, which you should record under two subcategories: a) how much compliance you achieved from your child, on a scale of 0 to 10, and b) how satisfied you were with the outcome, on a scale of 0 to 10. You may also want to write an actual description of the outcome, which would provide more information about what happened when you go back over your diary later.

The columns in your diary should look something like this:

Date	Situation	Anger Felt	Anger Expressed	Outcome
				a. Compliance **b.** Satisfaction

Keep the diary in this format for two weeks (you'll change the format later in the book). It will help you learn five things:

- How often you get angry.

- How intense your anger typically feels.

- How much you *modulate* you anger. The "Anger Felt" score minus the "Anger Expressed" score indicates the degree of modulation. Basically, this is how you tone down or soften the anger you feel when actually expressing it.

- How effective your anger is: Does it make your child listen and mind? Or does your child rage and rebel against your anger? Does your child *agree* to comply, but never follow through? Does your child comply, but only as long as you're watching?

- How satisfied you are with the outcome: Was the anger cost effective? Did you achieve what you wanted with minimum harm, or did your child seem hurt and disturbed by the experience?

Example

Patty, a working mother in her early thirties, came home to find that her nine-year-old son, Jason, had disregarded repeated requests to stay away from her drawing table. He'd used her mat knife to cut a picture out of a magazine and, in the process, had sliced one of her layouts underneath. She ran into the backyard and screamed at him in front of his neighborhood friends. Then she sent everyone home and banished Jason to his room with no TV privileges for the rest of the night. The following is the anger diary entry she made when she went to bed.

Date	Situation	Anger Felt	Anger Expressed	Outcome
8/17	Jason disturbed the things on my desk and ruined one of my layouts.	7	5	**a.** 9—He went straight to his room. **b.** 4—He needed to be punished but I felt bad about losing my temper.

3

Why You Get Angry

It was already 8:15 in the morning, and Jessica was still looking for her other shoe. The car had been warming up for a few minutes, and Jessica's father, Paul, was growing more and more impatient as he visualized the traffic building up on the bridge. He told Jessica to run and brush her teeth while he looked for her shoe. After checking under beds and in the closets, he finally found it behind the door in the bathroom. When he returned to the living room, he found Jessica spacing out watching cartoons, her teeth still unbrushed. It was the last straw. Paul made a big banging sound when he slammed the TV off and he yelled, "Get your teeth brushed and your jacket on in one minute or you're getting spanked—is that clear enough for you?"

Maria was having her usual check-in with her neighbor as she unloaded groceries from the car. As always, she kept a casual eye on her four-year-old son, Eddy, who was petting and playing with the next-door cat. Suddenly she heard a horn and whipped around in time to see Eddy throwing a rock at a passing car. Maria dropped the bags she was holding and grabbed her boy. Overwhelmed with fear and embarrassment, Maria shook Eddy repeatedly and screamed at him "You could cause an accident. Don't ever, ever, ever do that again!"

It was 5:30 on a hot afternoon. The kids were hungry, and the traffic was barely moving. Lynda tried to tune out the bickering between her two children, Derek and Tanya, by listening to the radio and singing along to herself. Lynda asked her kids what they wanted for dinner in an effort to deescalate what was turning into a full-blown argument in the back seat. But it was already too late. The yelling got louder, Derek hit Tanya, and Tanya's angry screaming filled the car. Before Lynda knew it, she was slamming on the brakes and shouting that if she heard one more sound, they would both go to bed without dinner.

Whether you are a single parent or you share parenting responsibilities with a partner, chances are you've had experiences similar to the ones described above. As a parent, you are exposed throughout the day to situations that test your patience and push your limits. If you were to ask Paul, Maria, or Lynda what made them so angry, you would get three very different responses. Paul's impatience to get going differs considerably from Maria's angry reaction to fear and embarrassment and from Lynda's exasperation at the end of a long day. But, despite obvious differences, all three share a common experience.

In this chapter you will learn the basic elements that exist in every angry situation. The two-step model of anger, described below, can illuminate not only the causes of anger but the important function that anger serves in reducing stress. The role of trigger thoughts in causing anger will be explained as we reexamine the experiences of Paul, Maria, and Lynda. Later in this chapter you'll get a chance to evaluate your own trigger thoughts while you learn new ways to cope with the everyday stresses of parenting.

The Two-Step Model of Anger

My own anger scares me sometimes. I wind up saying things I don't mean, and often doing things that I feel really guilty about later.

—Mother of two children, three and six years old

One thing that frustrates me is when I'm in a situation and I can feel myself getting more and more angry. I know I'm going to blow up—but even then, I can't seem to stop it from happening.

—Father of a nine-year-old boy

Anger is difficult for everyone. Parents who claim never to have felt out of control with anger are probably kidding themselves. Anger is a powerful emotion, as difficult to understand as it is to control. So an important first step in learning to control your anger is to find out where it comes from and how it works.

Two specific elements always precede an angry reaction: stress and trigger thoughts. Neither stress nor trigger thoughts alone are sufficient to create anger. Stress is the tinder, trigger thoughts are the match. You need both to kindle a fire. Recall the example of Paul, whose efforts to get out of the house turned into an angry confrontation with his daughter Jessica. Keeping in mind the two-step model of anger, you'll see how Paul's stress and trigger thoughts combined to cause his angry reaction that morning.

The presence of general underlying stress contributed a lot to Paul's frustration with Jessica. Before he took on his new role as a single dad, his performance at work had always been a top priority. He prided himself on the extra effort he put into projects, and his willingness to stay long hours when needed. Taking on the job of full-time parenting meant a big change in those priorities and an acceptance of new limitations at work. Paul was showing up late at the office more and more frequently these days, and he could sense his boss' disappointment. On this particular morning, Paul had made an extra effort to get started earlier than usual. His frustration peaked when he realized he was facing another late start—and another apology to his boss.

Although Paul's preexisting stress played a big role in creating his anger, the stress alone would not have caused his outburst. He might have felt anxious and frustrated, but not angry. The anger needed the help of a series of trigger thoughts that pushed Paul over the edge from worry and tension to anger.

As a last-ditch effort to speed things up, Paul thought he'd divide up the tasks with Jessica. He would find her other shoe, she would brush her teeth, and they would be on the road in less than five minutes. But, when he entered the living room, shoe in hand, to find Jessica still perched in front of the TV, his first thoughts were "She's purposely ignoring me" and "She should know better than to wait till the last second." With those thoughts his tension ignited into anger. He slammed off the TV and yelled a threat to get her moving.

The Function of Anger

There is an important reason why stress and anger are so closely related. Except when you are being physically threatened, the main function of anger is to alleviate stress. Anger can momentarily discharge or block awareness of painful levels of emotional or physical arousal (stress). As stress increases, discomfort increases as well. If stress levels get too high, it may feel intolerable, and anger is a quick method for discharging some of that mounting tension.

Recall the example of Maria, who had an immediate anger reaction when her son Eddy threw a rock at a passing car. This is an example of how quickly stress can turn to anger. The sound of the horn and the sight of her boy hurling the stone, caused an acute stress reaction that was almost immediately intolerable. Yelling at Eddy and grabbing his shoulders provided an outlet for the fear and embarrassment that flooded her.

Parental Stress

As a parent, you know that stress comes in many forms. Caring for children is not only an awesome responsibility, it's a job that requires total commitment, infinite patience, and constant attention. The following list from the book *When Anger Hurts* (McKay, Rogers, and McKay, 1989), describes the working conditions of your job as parent.

1. *Long hours.* You are "in charge" every hour of every day (including weekends and holidays). If you work outside the home, your parenting job starts well before you leave

the house in the morning and resumes the moment you come home. And it doesn't end at bedtime. Infants and babies may wake frequently during the night, and your sleep might be broken by a child who is ill or has a nightmare.

2. *Children are incredibly messy.* A lot of your time and energy is spent picking up, cleaning up, wiping up food, toys, clothing, and dirt spread throughout the house. Even parents of children who are responsible about cleaning up their own toys find themselves involved with encouraging, supervising, training, organizing, and supporting the cleanup effort.

3. *Children are noisy.* A household with children is a house filled with laughter, screaming, crying. Children are constantly asking questions. Any activity that requires quiet, such as reading, phone calls, or conversation, is always a struggle.

4. *Caring for children requires that you do many repetitive and time-consuming tasks.* The laundry, shopping, and cooking never end. Children need you to transport them everywhere—from sporting events and dance classes to the dentist.

5. *Children are self-centered.* They aren't usually aware that you are worn out, losing patience, or under a great deal of stress. Social skills, such as empathy or sensitivity to others, are learned over a long period of time.

6. *Children push the limits.* Normal children are constantly seeking autonomy. They want and need to do more for themselves, and they question your judgment and authority. From the two-year-old, who's just learned to say no, to the rebellious teen, children push and challenge the rules in order to grow up.

7. *Children need tremendous amounts of attention and approval.* They compete with anything and anyone that takes you away from them. Their attention-getting strategies may be

overt and obvious (look at me, see me, watch me), or co-
vert and indirect (sibling rivalry, destructive behavior, low
achievement at school).

8. *Children require vigilance.* They must be protected from immediate and potential dangers. Parents of young children
   must constantly watch them, staying alert for anything
   breakable, hot, sharp, or small enough to be swallowed.
   Parents of older children who play and travel away from
   home are always worried about bike or car accidents, the
   dangers of the playground, the dangers posed by strang-
   ers, and so on. No matter how vigilant you are, you never
   feel that your children are completely safe.

With all that to carry, it would be only fair if parents were
exempt from the other stresses in life. But being a parent is only
one of the roles that you fulfill. You also must face the everyday
stresses of being an adult in the world. While you juggle all your
parenting responsibilities, you may also be coping with problems
in a significant relationship, a painful separation, or lack of closeness. You may be experiencing problems in your workplace, re-
ceiving negative feedback from a supervisor, or having trouble
meeting deadlines. You may be experiencing physical stress in the
form of tense muscles, pain from illness or injury, or exhaustion.
Whatever you're facing in your life, it is important to recognize
that as a parent, and as an adult, you manage a tremendous number of responsibilities that inevitably create stress. Therefore, any
effort that you make to cope with anger must also include effective
strategies for coping with stress.

Trigger Thoughts

As you learned, stress by itself can't make you angry: Anger is a
two-step process. Stress is an important precursor to anger, but the
presence of trigger thoughts is a necessary second component of
the anger response.

Recall the example of Lynda, who was caught in traffic with
two kids fighting in the back seat. Lynda's physical discomfort—
the heat in the car, hunger, her fatigue from her day—and the

slow-moving traffic, contributed to a state of stressful arousal. As the noise from her children's bickering increased, so did her stress level. When Tanya began screaming, three trigger thoughts passed through Lynda's mind:

They both should know to keep quiet while I manage in this traffic.

They're doing this to drive me crazy.

They have no respect for each other or for me.

At the moment when Lynda stopped her car and shouted at her children, trigger thoughts had transformed her intolerable level of stress into anger. She now had a target for venting, which provided brief relief from her stress and mounting tension.

The assumption behind trigger thoughts is that a transgression has occurred: The child has been *bad* and therefore some kind of punishment is justified. Even if you know on an intellectual level that a certain trigger thought isn't true, when it passes through your mind during a state of stressful arousal, it feels true enough to set off an angry reaction. When Paul told himself "She's purposely ignoring me," the implication was that Jessica had deliberately delayed him by disregarding his requests. She was being bad and deserved punishment. When Lynda said to herself "They should know to keep quiet while I manage in this traffic," she was seeing Tanya and Derek as purposely disregarding a well-known rule of conduct in the car. They knew better and therefore should be punished. Trigger thoughts made it possible for Paul and Lynda to ignite high levels of stress into anger and vent it on their children. Their reactions were a consequence of the simple formula: Stress plus trigger thoughts equals anger.

Trigger Thoughts Can Change

You're doing last-minute shopping to prepare for a dinner party you're giving. The supermarket is crowded, and you're having trouble locating the things you need. After repeated reminders, your two-year-old continues to pull food off the shelves. This causes you some embarrassment and considerable delay as cereal boxes topple over each other and soup cans roll noisily across the aisle. Against her will, you put her in the child seat of the shopping cart to avoid more hassles. Moments later, you turn around to find she's opened a package of spaghetti and dumped hundreds of noodles all over the cart and floor.

Your response at a moment like this—whether you spank, yell, or hand your child something to play with while politely cleaning up the mess—will have a lot to do with the trigger thoughts you used when the spaghetti spilled. A trigger such as

> *I knew this would happen. She's getting me back for putting her in the cart seat.*

would likely incite more anger than

> *I should have left her with the neighbors. This is no place for a bored, over-tired two-year-old, especially when I'm in a rush.*

Given that the level of anger you experience toward your kids is directly affected by the kinds of trigger thoughts you use, one way to reduce your anger is to change your thinking patterns in difficult situations. An important first step toward anger control is to determine what kinds of trigger thoughts are most likely to get you mad.

The Parental Anger Survey

To determine which trigger thoughts are most associated with parental anger, we undertook a two-stage study. In the first stage we conducted in-depth interviews with thirty-five parents about the situations that make them angry and the methods they use to cope with those provocative situations. We also asked these parents to tell us what they were thinking during recent anger episodes with their children. The trigger thoughts they described became the basis for Stage Two of the study.

In Stage Two, we surveyed 250 parents who responded to our ads in national parenting magazines. Each participant was asked to read through a list of twenty-four common trigger thoughts (gleaned from the earlier interviews), and rate how often they tended to use each one. Next, they were asked to complete the

Parental Anger Inventory that you completed in chapter 2, as well as measures for the frequency and intensity of anger. This enabled us to find out which trigger thoughts were used more by parents with high levels of anger versus those with lower levels of anger.

In comparing the kinds of trigger thoughts parents used against their overall anger scores from the PAI, we found that people who feel more anger at their children use provoking trigger thoughts significantly more often. Of the twenty-four trigger thoughts included in our survey, eighteen were used much more frequently by parents with high levels of anger, compared to parents with lower anger levels.

When we examined the eighteen trigger thoughts more typical of high-anger parents, we found that they could be grouped into three main themes: (1) *assumed intent* (thinking that the child is misbehaving *deliberately* to upset you), (2) *magnification* (in your mind, making the situation worse than it really is), and (3) *labeling* (using negative, pejorative words to describe the child, or his or her behavior).

Our findings suggest that trigger thoughts are an important factor in increasing the frequency and intensity of your anger toward your children. While chapter 5 will give you step-by-step help in changing and reducing your trigger thoughts, the first step is to learn how to identify them.

Recognizing Your Trigger Thoughts

Below is a list of the eighteen trigger thoughts associated with high levels of anger. For now, read through the list and see whether any of these thoughts seem familiar—perhaps thoughts you've had during various angry episodes with your child.

Here are the eighteen trigger thoughts, grouped in the three categories.

Assumed Intent

_____   1.   You're doing it to annoy me.

_____   2.   You're defying me.

_____   3.   You're trying to drive me crazy.

_____ 4. You're trying to test me (see how far you can go).

_____ 5. You're tuning me out intentionally.

_____ 6. You're taking advantage of me.

_____ 7. You're doing this deliberately (to get back at me, hurt me, spite me, etc.).

Magnification

_____ 8. I can't stand it.

_____ 9. This behavior is intolerable.

_____ 10. You've gone too far this time.

_____ 11. You never listen.

_____ 12. How dare you (look at me like that, talk to me like that, do that, etc.).

_____ 13. You turn everything into a (power struggle, fight, lousy time together, nightmare, etc.).

Labeling

_____ 14. You're getting out of control.

_____ 15. This is manipulation.

_____ 16. You're so (lazy, malicious, stubborn, disrespectful, ungrateful, willful, selfish, cruel, stupid, bratty, spoiled, contrary, etc.).

_____ 17. You're deliberately being mean, a jerk, etc.

_____ 18. You don't care (what happens, how I feel, who you hurt, etc.).

Now look back at the entries in your anger diary, and try to recall which of the trigger thoughts in the list you may have used during any of those recent episodes. Pay particular attention to any trigger thoughts you had on more than one occasion. You may use many different trigger thoughts depending on the situation, or a very few may seem to come up over and over again.

Keeping in mind what you've learned from reviewing your anger diary, read through the list of trigger thoughts again. This time put a check mark next to the triggers that you remember having at least once. If any of the trigger thoughts stand out as ones that you've used often, mark them with a star. Remember, this list only represents a small number of trigger thoughts and may not include the thoughts that you use most frequently. However, because of their relationship to high anger levels in parents, the trigger thoughts in this list should be given special attention as you learn more about identifying and changing your thinking patterns in stressful situations.

Adding to Your Anger Diary

Now that you've learned about the role trigger thoughts play in sparking anger, you'll need to practice identifying your own use of trigger thoughts on a day-to-day basis. So far, your anger diary has allowed you to track every anger episode with your child. By measuring your own anger levels in different situations and then noting the outcome, you're getting a clearer picture of the effect that anger has in your daily life. Now you can start to include your own thoughts as you record episodes in your anger diary. From this point on, your diary entries should include a column for recording trigger thoughts. Your new diary entries should look something like this:

Date	Situation	Trigger Thought(s)	Anger Felt	Anger Expressed	Outcome
					a. Compliance
					b. Satisfaction

Example

Keith got home late from a meeting to discover that the babysitter had forgotten to make dinner for his daughter, who had been lightly snacking on chips all evening long. Tired out and still feeling anxious from his meeting, he scanned the fridge for something quick and easy to make for dinner. Twenty minutes later he called his daughter in for a dinner of macaroni and cheese and hot dogs. As soon as she sat down, the complaints started. She wasn't really hungry; she had hot dogs yesterday; the macaroni wasn't cooked enough; they weren't the kind of hot dogs she liked. Keith was irritated that she had filled up on junk food and now was giving him a hard time on top of it. He contained his temper and insisted that she eat. But when she pushed the plate away in protest, knocking over her glass of milk, he lost it. He picked her up from the table, carried her to her room, tossed her onto the bed, and slammed the door. Later that night, Keith made the following entry.

Date	Situation	Trigger Thoughts	Felt Anger	Expressed Anger	Outcome
6/12	Rachel snacked on chips all night and then refused to eat the dinner I made for her. She complained a lot and spilled milk all over the table.	You only think about yourself. You deliberately made a mess to get back at me.	8	8	**a.** 5—She was so angry when I pushed her around that she didn't get the point about dinner. **b.** 3—I felt awful about blowing up, but it was also a relief to get some quiet so I could calm down.

4

Why Kids Act the Way
They Do

To understand why the trigger thoughts that elicit parental anger are dangerous distortions, it's necessary to first understand what makes kids act the way they do.

According to our study, the trigger thoughts that were most related to anger assumed that the child had deliberately set out to provoke the parent. "You're deliberately being mean," "You're taking advantage of me," "You're trying to test me," are some examples of triggers that *assume intent*. Most parents attribute motives to their children, especially when the child is misbehaving or when the parent is confused by the child's behavior. They often assume that their child is doing it to "get at" them.

Are children really misbehaving just to annoy their parents? Researchers and child development specialists find that this is rarely the case. Torturing parents is not often a motive for kids. Instead, there appear to be four major factors that influence a child's behavior: (1) the child's temperament, (2) the age-appropriate behaviors and the developmental challenges facing the child at different stages, (3) the child's needs and coping strategies for meeting those needs, and (4) the role of reinforcement in maintaining unwanted behaviors.

Temperament

No two babies are the same. Each is born with his or her own set of physical features (hair color, eye color, shape of mouth, size of nose, height, weight, body type and proportions). Similarly, babies are born with major differences in their temperament. Mothers often state that each of their children was different from day one— and they're right. *Temperament* refers to the built-in wiring that each child is issued at (or before) birth—the way he or she tends to respond to life experiences. How does your child react to disappointment? Does he or she recover quickly, sulk and whine for a while, or throw a tantrum that lasts for an hour? Temperament determines these patterns.

The Traits That Make Up Temperament

Temperament isn't reflected in behavior that occurs once or twice, randomly, but in behavior that occurs in a pattern—that is consistent over time. Temperament is innate: It's not a product of the environment, your responses, nor of your child's attempts to elicit some response from you.

A child's temperament can be thought of as a constellation of nine different characteristics, all significant to the child's experience of life and to your experience of the child. Each child will have each of the nine traits in different proportions, and depending on that unique mix, a child can be happy or moody, full of energy or quiet, stubborn or acquiescent, easy to live with or extremely difficult to enjoy.

The nine characteristics that determine temperament (adapted from Turecki and Tonner 1985) are listed below. As you read the list, you may want to think about how each of these traits is demonstrated in your child.

- **Activity level.** How much activity or restlessness does the child show generally, from a very early age? How much spontaneous movement? A child with this trait at a difficult level would be very active and restless, fidgety—a child who never slows down and hates to be confined.

- **Quality of mood.** How would you describe the child's basic disposition? Positive and happy or negative, fussy, and serious? A child with this trait at a difficult level would be cranky or serious—a child who doesn't seem to get much pleasure from life.

- **Approach/withdrawal.** How does the child respond to new experiences (people, food, places, clothes, activities)? Does he or she approach with enthusiasm or withdraw in fear? A child with this trait at a difficult level would be shy and clingy—a child who stubbornly refuses to go forward into new situations.

- **Rhythmicity.** How regular is the child in eating, sleeping, and bowel habits? A child with this trait at a difficult level would get hungry and tired at unpredictable times, making regular mealtimes and bedtimes a source of conflict.

- **Adaptability.** How does the child adapt to transition and change? A child with this trait at a difficult level would be tremendously resistant to changes in activity, routine, food, or clothing—a child who is inflexible and very particular.

- **Sensory threshold.** How does the child react to changes and differences in the environment, to sensory stimuli such as noise, light, smells, tastes, pain, weather, wet diapers? Does he or she get perturbed or overstimulated easily? A child with this trait at a difficult level would be sensitive to physical stimuli and easily bothered—by the way food smells, the way clothes feel, the brightness of lights, the loudness of noises.

- **Intensity of reaction.** How intense (loud) is the child's reaction to both positive and negative stimuli? A child

with this trait at a difficult level would be loud and forceful, whether he or she is happy, sad, or angry.

- **Distractibility.** How easily distracted is the child, particularly when upset? Can he or she pay attention? A child
  with this trait at a difficult level would have difficulty
  concentrating and paying attention, would daydream instead of listening, and would tend to forget instructions.

- **Persistence.** How long can the child remain focused on
  one thing? When happily engaged in an activity, does he
  or she stay with it for a long time? When unhappy, does
  he or she persist stubbornly with attempts to get his or her
  needs met? A child with this trait at a difficult level would
  be extremely stubborn, wouldn't give up, and might persevere with a tantrum for an hour.

It's not hard to see how these biological differences might
affect the child's experience of life. And it's not difficult to imagine
how the child's temperament would, in turn, affect the way a parent responds to the child. This is even more true when a child has
one or more of the traits described above at a difficult level or
when the individual traits interact so as to create difficulties. For
example, an extremely irritable child (negative quality of mood)
who cries easily (low sensory threshold) and is less easily placated
(low distractibility) would be harder to parent than a child with a
sunny disposition who is less sensitive to stimuli and easily distracted from upsets. Similarly, a child with a very high activity
level will likely get into things more, turn the house upside down,
and need more supervision and limit setting than a child who isn't
constantly on the move.

The "fit" between the parent's temperament and the child's
also affects the relationship. A child who reacts intensely in all situations would be even more difficult for the parent who has a low
sensory threshold or a negative mood. A very shy or timid child
with a low activity level may be more disappointing and frustrat-
ing for a parent who is highly active and enjoys new situations.

It is still largely unsolved whether these temperamental patterns are hereditary or are caused by environmental influences on

the developing fetus. In either case, it is important to realize that these characteristics are neither bad nor good. They are simply differences like eye or hair color. Children don't manifest temperamental differences in order to make their parents' lives more difficult. They are born with them, and they have no choice but to express them.

Age-Appropriate Behaviors and Developmental Challenges

As children grow and develop, they pass through many stages, each of which is characterized by typical behaviors. To understand why your child may be acting a certain way, you need to be familiar with these stages and behaviors. Most parents, for example, have heard of the "terrible twos," so they're not totally surprised when they begin to hear the word "No!" on a regular basis and to experience temper tantrums on a (hopefully) less regular basis. But many parents are unaware that somewhat similar behavior can occur in children as young as ten or eleven months—and be perfectly appropriate. And what about children aged three, five, or seven? What's typical behavior for those ages?

Since every child is an individual, with different characteristics and different rates of development, no description of "typical" behaviors will fit each child perfectly. Temperament plays a huge part in the degree to which many age-typical behaviors are manifested. Nonetheless, some general developmental guidelines can be described, as we have done in the sections that follow. (The material in these sections is adapted from the books on age-appropriate behaviors by Louise Ames, Frances Ilg, and Carol Chase Haber listed in the reference section at the end of the book.)

The One-Year-Old

Jack is a fairly typical one-year-old. His most conspicuous characteristic is his almost complete egocentricity: He's all take and no give. He insists on having his own way, becomes grabby about possessions, wants everything for himself alone. He simply cannot share. Even when playing in a group, Jack's play is solitary. He's stubborn, and violent displays of temper over the least frustration are normal. Now that he's upright and walking, the world is his to discover, so he runs around poking, prodding, pushing, and tasting everything he can get his hands on.

The struggle for autonomy is the major developmental challenge at this age. Jack is completely focused on testing his parents' limits and discovering his own. He's defiant, tremendously impulsive, and doesn't know the difference between good and bad. He says "no" instead of "yes," "up" instead of "down." At the same time, he clings to his mother, almost desperately at times. No matter how good the relationship with the parent, this is an age where things tends to be difficult. (Ames, Ilg, and Haber 1982)

The Two-Year-Old

Life for two-year-old Marisa is actually a little easier than when she was one. Now she can walk and run and climb and she can express her needs more clearly. Her two most conspicuous characteristics are a tremendous demand for sameness and a tremendous difficulty making decisions. This is possibly the worst age of all for making choices. As soon as Marisa settles on one option she immediately wants the other. She also has a complete inability to modulate: no volume control (over her voice), no emotional control, no physical control. She continues to explore everything by touch, taste, and smell. She asks "why" to every statement out of her mother's mouth, but it's a request for more information, not an attempt to resist or drive her mother crazy. She enjoys other children, though she has no empathy and she more often is simply playing alongside others rather than truly playing *with* them. She still doesn't share her toys much.

At two-and-a-half, Marisa experiences violent, demanding, explosive emotions. Frequent temper tantrums are characteristic. She wants whatever she isn't getting, and she may attempt to manipulate to get her own way, pitting one parent against the other. She whines, hits, kicks, and punches to get what she wants. This is not true aggressiveness, however, she's just acting out strong drives for her desires. She's bossy and demanding—not to be deliberately obnoxious—but because she is unsure of herself. The world seems big and dangerous; if she can control or command even a small part of it (her parents), it helps her feel secure. (Ames and Ilg 1976)

The Three-Year-Old

Daniel is a typical three-year-old. His most conspicuous characteristic is the expressed desire for "we-ness." "Let's go play" is a common refrain. He wants to help his mother with the housework, go shopping with her, play with her—basically to please her. Because his body is more under his control, he has begun to develop a sense of his competence. He's much less selfish and less dependent on his mother. Daniel enjoys playing with other children and can actually share at times, though his anger and frustration may still become physical. He experiences lots of fantasy activities—at times he can't differentiate between fantasy and reality. He has an imaginary companion (under his control), and sometimes he pretends to be someone other than himself.

At three-and-a-half, life becomes more difficult for Daniel. The struggle for autonomy reasserts itself. He wants to strengthen his will; he is determined and very assertive. Intense conflict becomes inevitable, but he's also very insecure emotionally because of his growing recognition of his separateness from others. He stutters, stumbles, sucks his thumb, and express fears of things that didn't used to scare him. Once again he tries to overcome the insecurity by dominating his parents: "Don't look," "Don't laugh," "Don't talk," he orders. (Ames and Ilg 1985)

The Four-Year-Old

The outstanding trait of four-year-old Sophie is her love of going out of bounds. She hits, kicks, and spits if aroused and has even tried to run away from home when things didn't please her. She laughs hilariously, cries loudly, and can be extremely silly. She loves a lot and hates a lot and in general has extremely volatile emotions. Sophie's verbal "out of boundness" is manifested by exaggerating, boasting, and swaggering. She enjoys using vulgar words and especially enjoys watching her parents' expressions while she uses them.

Sophie still loves fantasies and tells tall tales with regularity, but she's not lying; she's just struggling with her ability to distinguish fact from fantasy. However, she sometimes does lie to avoid punishment, if she thinks that what she did is worse than lying. She believes that possession means ownership, but she's not a thief. Sophie is often rude to her parents—she's challenging their authority and testing the limits of her independence. She doesn't understand morality and obeys rules out of fear of punishment. She can be aggressive with her siblings, and her mother doesn't trust her alone with the baby. Paradoxically, Sophie still likes boundaries and limits, since sometimes her expansiveness seems a little too much even for her. (Ames and Ilg 1976)

The Five-Year-Old

The challenge for Max, a typical five-year-old, seems to be how to be good. He works hard at it, and for the most part he succeeds. His mother is the center of his world; he wants to please her, be near her, and help her. He's quieter and is more interested in the familiar than in the new and strange and exciting. He's more secure, more serious, not much of a worrier.

At five-and-a-half, autonomy becomes an issue again. Max is brash, combative, and defiant. He doesn't always openly defy his parents, but instead he will dawdle—with the same result. He has tantrums and sulks; sometimes he complains of headaches, colds, and stomach aches. Most importantly, he still needs and requests reassurance, asking "Do you love me?" (Ames and Ilg 1979a)

The Six-Year-Old

The most conspicuous trait for six-year-old Olivia is ambivalence. Whatever she does, she does the opposite just as readily. Whatever she wants, she wants the opposite as well. She changes her mind all the time about little things. About big things, she has a hard time making up her mind. But once made up, it's hard for her to change it. Olivia is more closely involved with her mother than at any other age, but there is great ambivalence in this relationship too. She is beginning to really separate from her mother and wants to be independent, but she wants to be close as well. Anything that goes wrong is taken out on her mother.

Her emerging independence is very anxiety provoking. To cope with the anxiety, Olivia attempts desperately to be in control: to be best, to be first, to have the most of everything, to be loved and praised. She can't bear to lose in a competitive situation, has a constant desire to be noticed, and is very sensitive to criticism. Her feelings get hurt very easily, and she cries easily about emotional as well as physical hurts. She's not always honest and doesn't always tell the truth. She's really fresh. She's also oppositional, violent, and loud. Yet her insecurity is manifested at the same time by her asking, "Even though I've been bad, do you still love me?" Olivia's playtimes are stormy because her need to be first and to win create difficulties. With younger siblings she's bossy; she argues, teases, bullies, frightens, torments, gets angry, and hits. (Ames and Ilg 1979b)

The Seven-Year-Old

As a typical seven-year-old, Jason's most conspicuous characteristic is his tendency toward perseveration: going on and on with a task or situation until it is completed to his satisfaction or until somebody stops him. His expectations of himself are high—often too high. He wants to be perfect and is ashamed of any mistakes. In general, seven is an age of withdrawal, of pulling in, of calming down, of discovering who is inside. Jason lives in a world of thought, observing the outside world and then thinking about what he's observed. His tendency to withdraw is seen particularly when things get tough. He worries about everything, more than at any other age. He worries about being late for school (even though this has never happened); he worries about the possibility of war; he worries about someone dying. He's afraid of the dark.

Jason doesn't like many people, thinks they're mean or unfriendly. He feels that his parents like his brothers and sisters more than they like him. "Nobody likes me—I might as well be dead" is sometimes heard. His characteristic expression is a frown. And although tears come easily, he's embarrassed to cry in front of other people. He's easily disappointed and sulking: Pouting and general moodiness are normal expressions of his age. (Ames and Haber 1976)

The Eight-Year-Old

Devon is a typical eight-year-old. Her most distinguishing characteristic is the speed with which she does everything. She zooms around the house or yard, eats fast, reads fast, talks fast, plays fast. She's outgoing, likes attention, and is very interested in human relationships—to the point of being downright nosy. Devon's relationships with friends and family are important to her, but her most intense connection is with her mother. She can't seem to get enough of her mother's attention, is highly possessive of her, and wants to hang around her all the time. This possessiveness and jealousy makes her relationships with her siblings difficult. Devon tends to judge people—especially herself. She's too aware of her own failures and is hard on herself for them. She's hard on others as well, quarrelsome and aggressive, particularly with her mother. At the same time, her feelings are easily hurt, and she is sensitive to being judged by others. (Ames and Haber 1989)

The Nine-Year-Old

Ryan, a typical nine-year-old, is most characterized by his emergence from his strong preoccupation with his mother. Instead of not getting enough of her, sometimes he resents her presence. In fact he often seems so preoccupied with his own activities that he doesn't even hear her talking to him. He more or less ignores her. He reacts negatively to her demands for neatness and cleanliness. He's also more distant from his father and resents being bossed. He rebels against his parents' authority by looking right through them while they're giving a command, by complaining while carrying out their command, or by actively resisting. Fighting and bickering are common, as are name calling and even wrestling.

Ryan is a self-starter, and once started, wants to continue in his own way, at his own pace, in his own direction. He takes himself very seriously and wants to do things just right, not just for praise, but also for inner satisfaction. His willpower is strong. Ryan has wide mood swings, and his emotional responses are unpredictable. He worries and complains and is very concerned with what's fair and unfair. Nine is an age where individual differences show more than at other ages. For example, some kids love money, others are indifferent; some have small appetites, others eat anything; some adore blood and guts and violence in movies, others hate it; some are good with their hands, others are awkward. (Ames and Haber 1990)

Needs and Coping Strategies

It has been asserted (Dreikurs 1964; Dinkmeyer and McKay 1983) that a child's strongest motivation is the desire to belong in his or her family. For the child to feel that sense of belonging, the contribution he or she makes to the family must be noticed and validated. In other words, the child must feel significant because of who he or she is. This sense of belonging is the source of all security, so everything the child does—including misbehaving—is aimed at finding his or her place and feeling significant in the family. From a very young age, children observe their families to figure out how to belong. How they try to achieve significance depends on many factors, including their skills, observations, environment, and position in the family.

Children are usually excellent observers. Unfortunately their interpretation of events may not be accurate, which can lead to mistaken beliefs about how best to achieve significance in the family.

For example, Brian had just turned four when his baby sister Becky was born. He accurately observed that Becky got a lot of attention when she cried or dirtied her diapers. He knew that the attention given to Becky used to be his, and he perceived—mistakenly—that he had lost his place in the family and needed to find a way to regain his significance. Brian concluded that only by behaving like baby Becky (by crying, whining, wetting himself) could he regain his sense of belonging. Thus he started "misbehaving" or "regressing" in order to achieve that goal.

The family environment, its values and attitudes, can also determine the method a child chooses for achieving significance. Brian's family valued education, and that value was communicated to him in many ways. Over time, Brian mistakenly came to believe that the *only* way to achieve significance was to excel, to be the best, at play and at school. He worried and struggled to maintain a standard of excellence that he thought was his only path to belonging.

Family position plays a part as well. When Becky, Brian's sister, was little, she saw Brian in the role of "good student." Seeing what that put Brian through, Becky decided that it took too much work and she didn't want to bother. Since the good-student role had already been taken, the only available option was the role of "bad student," the one who fails all her classes despite her intelligence. Had Becky had a different temperament (she was easily distracted and not persistent), she might have tried to surpass her older brother and rob Brian of his perceived role.

If children can feel a sense of significance and belonging through their competence and participation in the family, then they grow and flourish. Three-year-old Jamie feels this sense of competence and belonging. When his dad tends the vegetable garden, Jamie takes his miniature shovel and helps him dig. He helps his mom choose the vegetables for dinner and carries them to the table when dinner is ready. When he's finished eating, he asks to be excused and takes his own plate into the kitchen. His parents try to acknowledge and appreciate his help and express that appreciation to him. And though limits are clearly set when Jamie challenges his parents' authority, those challenges are seen as normal expressions of his developing autonomy. Under these conditions, Jamie will thrive.

Unfortunately, children can become easily discouraged in their natural attempts to achieve a sense of significance. They still experience a desperate need to belong but can't find a way to feel important in the family. Three-year-old Sarah is well on the way to feeling discouraged. She wants to help her mom with the household chores, but every time she offers to help, her mother says "No." No, she's too little to use the broom. No, she'll break the china with the duster. No, she'll make too much mess in the kitchen. Furthermore, when Sarah challenges her parents' limits, she is punished and made to feel like a bad person. Sarah notices that her contributions are neither acknowledged nor validated. She doesn't feel a sense of belonging or significance in the family.

Three Misdirected Goals

When a child's attempts to achieve significance through his or her own contributions fail, he or she has to find alternate routes to getting those needs met, since they are fundamental to the child's sense of safety, security, and self-esteem. In frustration, the child may try to get his or her parents' attention, try to achieve some power in the family, or, as a last resort, try to get back at them.

Attention

Since Sarah can't get recognition for her efforts to contribute positively to the family, she may decide that misbehaving is a more effective way to get the attention she needs. The goal of attention for attention's sake takes the place of the goal of positive contribution. As the center of attention, Sarah reasons, she may attain some significance and a sense of belonging. This mistaken belief then comes to govern much of her behavior. She'll become desperate for attention and develop great skill in increasing family upsets.

Power

A child's desperate attempts to be the center of attention are usually met with disapproval. Parents may try forcibly to thwart these demands for attention, so once again the child will have to find an alternate way to feel significant. Observing the power inherent in her parents' forceful behavior, Sarah may decide that by attaining such power herself she can achieve significance. She may try to feel powerful by refusing requests and defying the rules. Then everything starts to become a nearly life-and-death struggle for control. Sarah hasn't been able to achieve recognition through her attempts at contributing positively, nor through her more direct attempts to gain attention. Attaining power feels like the only option.

Revenge

Faced with a challenge to their authority, parents often respond by escalating the struggle—even to the point of physical force. As this pattern intensifies, the child may become further discouraged. His or her attempts to attain significance through power have failed, just like the previous attempts to gain attention and make positive contributions. Hurt and angry at being thwarted in every attempt, the child may decide that the only way to be noticed is to strike back. Revenge becomes the chosen way to achieve significance. Every time the child feels hurt, he or she tries to inflict pain on the parents in return.

Other Needs

In each of the preceding cases, the child's "misbehavior" can be seen in the context of his or her attempts to meet a fundamental need: to achieve a necessary significance, to feel important, to establish a place in his or her family, to belong. To fill this need, the child does whatever he or she thinks will work. At a less fundamental level, every child has a multitude of needs. These range from the broad needs for autonomy and worth to the everyday needs for sleep, food, time to calm down when overstimulated, physical nurturing (hugs, kisses, caresses), and safety (through parents' application of clear limits). These needs change from year to year, from day to day, and from minute to minute.

Although they are unlikely to be the cause of recurrent problems, in any particular situation these needs can contribute to the child's behavior. If the child is tired, he or she will be less likely to comply with requests in a timely manner, more readily frustrated, and more easily overstimulated. Hunger can also exert an influence in similar ways. Meeting these everyday needs can make it easier to address the more fundamental needs described earlier.

For example, May always did her grocery shopping at the end of the day. She picked up Scott from preschool and headed straight for the supermarket. Nearly every trip was a nightmare. Scott insisted on hanging off the side of the cart or, worse, pushing it himself and racing up and down the aisles. He pulled items off the shelves randomly or wandered away from her and refused to come when she called. Once, out of frustration, May opened a box of crackers and offered one to Scott, to bribe him into sitting cooperatively in the cart. He ate a few and calmed down considerably. He was hungry.

Scott's acting out didn't cease completely when his need for food was met. However, it noticeably decreased, and May could then decide how to address the remainder of Scott's problem behavior from the perspective of his more fundamental needs.

Reinforcement

It's well known that if you reward a child for doing something, he or she is more likely to do it again. Almost equally well known is that if you completely ignore a child when he or she does something, that behavior is likely to disappear over time. Humans are biologically designed to seek pleasure and avoid pain. From the earliest experiences a child learns that pleasure is associated with the nurturing parent. Thus, over time, the parent becomes inherently rewarding and can eventually reinforce a child's behavior simply by noticing it. This happens when the attention is positive: a smile, a nod, a friendly or supportive comment. It also happens when the attention is negative: yelling, scolding, even hitting.

In the absence of positive attention, children find negative attention very reinforcing. This makes the task of disciplining your child a complex one, since even your negative responses to your child's misbehavior can act as reinforcement and increase the likelihood that the behavior will be repeated. You may be reinforcing your child's misbehavior without even realizing it. So almost the only way not to reinforce a behavior is to completely ignore it. (An alternative approach is discussed in chapter 7.)

Another way a child's behavior can be inadvertently reinforced is through the process of identification. This process can be seen most commonly in children imitating their parent's behavior. Your child probably imitates things you say and do, and such imitation is inherently rewarding to the child, and thus reinforcing of the behavior. For instance, a child's willingness to experiment with drugs may be reinforced by observations of a parent's liberal use of alcohol. Shoplifting jaunts may be inadvertently reinforced by observing a parent removing the hotel ashtrays or towels. Lying may be reinforced by hearing the parent fudge the truth about the child's age to purchase a less expensive airline or movie ticket.

How Do You Reinforce Behaviors?

As a parent, it's your job to determine what you might be doing to reinforce your child's unwanted behaviors. Here's a short exercise to help you.

Draw a line down the center of a piece of paper. On the left, write your child's most aggravating and common misbehavior. On the right, jot down your typical response(s) to that behavior. Now think carefully what part of that response could be rewarding to your child. All it takes is a smile behind your stern words, a spontaneous thought that your child is a chip off the old block, or a scolding that delivers more attention than the child has had all day from you.

Next ask yourself what other rewards might exist for the misbehavior. Does it reduce the child's anxiety, get attention from friends, allow him or her to avoid something unpleasant? Is the misbehavior itself fun? Does the behavior allow the child to feel closer to you (is it something you do in some fashion)? Also, are there any consequences for the misbehavior? If not, there's no reason for the child to stop it. Or are the consequences occasional and intermittent? If so, the child will likely take a chance, thinking he or she may escape a strong response this time.

Typical Problems Facing Parents

The Parental Anger Inventory that you completed in chapter 2 included fifty examples of problem situations that might evoke an angry response in parents. In our survey, twenty of those problem situations, listed below, were marked significantly more often by parents who had high levels of anger versus those with lower anger levels. (In the list, the numbers in parentheses correspond to the numbers in the questionnaire you completed in chapter 2.)

1. (2.) You ask your child to do something and he or she won't do it.

2. (7.) Your child does something (plays with something of yours or goes outside) without asking permission.

3. (8.) You tell your child to do something and he or she says "I already did" when you know this is not true.

4. (13.) Your child screams and yells when you say "no" after he or she asks for something in a store or at home.

5. (14.) Your child screams and yells at his or her sisters and/or brothers.

6. (16.) Your child bothers you when you are busy working or talking.

7. (18.) Your child breaks things on purpose.

8. (19.) Your child doesn't listen to you in public.

9. (20.) Your child uses curse words when he or she talks to you.

10. (23.) Your child says things that are not true on purpose.

11. (25.) Your child plays too loudly.

12. (28.) Your child takes things that don't belong to him or her.

13. (29.) Your child won't answer you when you ask him or her a question.

14. (31.) Your child demands something immediately.

15. (33.) Your child does not share toys.

16. (34.) Your child interrupts you when you are talking with someone.

17. (36.) Your child constantly touches things when you are in a store.

18. (39.) Your child screams, yells, and/or gets in fights during car trips.

19. (44.) Your child doesn't do his or her chores.

20. (45.) Your child misbehaves after you have had a bad day.

What makes these situations especially upsetting are trigger thoughts that assume intent, magnify, or label the child or his or her behavior in a negative way. It would make a big difference in your level of anger if you could replace those triggers with a new explanation of your child's behavior—one based on an understanding of his or her temperament, age-appropriate behaviors, need for belonging and significance, and the role of reinforcement. This new, more accurate interpretation of your child's behavior can help you let go of the feeling that he or she is being bad and doing terrible, unacceptable things. It can help you to stay calm and deal with the problem in a way you won't regret.

The following pages provide an analysis of each of the twenty most anger-provoking situations. Use these pages as a reference; look through them to find those problem behaviors that are relevant in your family. (The numbers correspond to those in the list above.) For each problem situation, a typical trigger thought is suggested, followed by an alternative explanation of the child's behavior that takes into account the four factors of temperament, developmental appropriateness, needs and coping strategies, and reinforcement. These factors provide the understanding necessary for reinterpreting your child's behavior in a way that won't trigger anger.

It's assumed in these examples that the problem behavior occurs consistently, rather than as a single, random event. This consistency provides the context for understanding the contributions of temperament as well as the role of the child's underlying need to achieve a sense of significance and belonging.

After you have read the pages that correspond to situations that occur between you and your child, turn to page 86 and do the exercise that appears there. It will help you continue to look at the angry episodes between you and your child in terms of the knowledge you have gained in this chapter.

1. (2.) *You ask your child to do something and he or she won't do it.*

Typical Trigger Thoughts

Assumed intent: "You're deliberately defying me."

Magnification: "This is horrible."

Labeling: "You're such a brat."

Alternative Explanations

Temperament: A child whose activity level is extremely high may simply be too busy to do what you ask. A high distractibility level may make it hard for the child to attend to or remember your request. If your request involves a change in the child's current activity, a difficulty adapting to transitions would affect his or her response. Finally, if the lack of response is a challenge to your authority, a high level of persistence would cause the child to persevere with the challenge.

Developmentally appropriate behaviors: Resisting parents' requests is a developmentally normal part of children's struggle for autonomy. The struggle asserts itself more forcefully in the second half of each year (two-and-a-half, three-and-a-half). Children whose efforts at independence have been consistently thwarted may feel the need even more strongly—and therefore may challenge even more.

Needs and coping strategies: As a recurrent behavior this suggests a consistent pattern of unmet fundamental needs. The child may have felt unable to attain significance through positive contributions or efforts to be the center of attention, and may now be attempting to win power in order to feel significant. This would prolong and exacerbate any age-appropriate challenges to authority.

Reinforcement: If the child has been reinforced in the past for refusing to comply with your requests, he or she may simply be responding to your teaching. For example, if when your child doesn't do what you ask within a few minutes you give up and do the task yourself, this reinforces the child's refusal. If you nag, your child may feel he or she has gained needed, albeit negative, attention. If your child regularly asks you to do things for him or her that you refuse, he or she may be imitating your behavior, which is inherently reinforcing

2. (7.) *Your child does something (plays with something of yours or goes outside) without asking permission.*

Typical Trigger Thoughts

Assumed intent: "You know this is wrong and you're doing it anyway."

Magnification: "I hate it when you do this."

Labeling: "You're so disobedient."

Alternative Explanations

Temperament: A high level of distractibility would make it more difficult for the child to remember to ask permission or to remember whether he or she did already ask. A high activity level, coupled with a tendency to approach new situations without fear, increases the likelihood of this behavior.

Developmentally appropriate behaviors: Developing autonomy and independence requires that children test limits and challenge authority. Doing something without asking permission is a developmentally normal attempt to do that. From ages two through five, children want to touch everything; they love new things and new challenges and believe that possession means ownership.

Needs and coping strategies: A child who has felt unable to achieve a significant place in the family through his or her own contributions and competence will need to find another way to meet that need. The child may be attempting to achieve significance through power, and will thus persevere in an attempt to challenge your authority (by not asking your permission) as a way of meeting this need. This would obviously exacerbate any age-appropriate expressions of the need for independence and autonomy.

Reinforcement: If you believe that it's OK to use your child's possessions without asking, your child may be imitating that behavior when he or she plays with something of yours without asking, which is inherently rewarding. If he or she has gone outside on occasion without asking without repercussion, you may have reinforced that behavior by implying that it is acceptable. Any negative attention that the child receives when he or she does something without asking permission can also be reinforcing, especially in the absence of consistent positive attention.

3. (8.) You tell your child to do something and he or she says "I already did" when you know this is not true.

Typical Trigger Thoughts

Assumed intent: "You're trying to drive me crazy."

Magnification: "I can't stand this."

Labeling: "You're such a brat."

Alternative Explanations

Temperament: The two traits most likely to contribute to this behavior are distractibility and persistence. A child who forgets easily and is easily distracted might actually think a task has been completed when it has not. Strong, negative persistence will increase the chances of the child maintaining his or her story in the face of your disbelief (or proof).

Developmentally appropriate behaviors: Challenging your authority in this way is a typical means of establishing autonomy for children of all ages. Typical for four-year-olds, whose out-of-boundness is the order of the day, is lying to avoid punishment or disapproval. At five-and-a-half, this is a manifestation of age-appropriate oppositional behavior. At six, lying—especially about accomplishments—is often a part of the desire to seem the best.

Needs and coping strategies: This behavior may reflect the child's need for power as a way of feeling significant. Or it may reflect a strategy for coping with feelings of insignificance or low self-esteem. If the situation routinely occurs when the child is tired, fatigue and the accompanying desire to avoid doing the requested task may also exacerbate this behavior.

Reinforcement: If the goal of the child's behavior is to demonstrate his or her power, engaging in a power struggle to prove otherwise or to force him or her to do what you ask will reinforce the behavior.

4. (13.) *Your child screams and yells when you say "no" after he or she asks for something in a store or at home.*

Typical Trigger Thoughts

Assumed intent: "You're trying to humiliate me."

Magnification: "I can't stand it."

Labeling: "You're so manipulative."

Alternative Explanations

Temperament: Quality of mood, intensity of reaction, and persistence are the traits most likely to influence this behavior. A child with a disposition that's serious and hard to please will react more negatively to disappointment than a child with a sunnier disposition. If the child has a high intensity of reaction coupled with high persistence, the screams and yells will be loud and long.

Developmentally appropriate behaviors: When children want something, they want it now. And when frustrated, they show their dissatisfaction and disappointment in the way that's most typical of their age and most likely to get them what they want. For example, a two-year-old's screams of frustration are a normal manifestation of the inability to modulate his or her reactions. At age four, verbal out-of-boundness is the age-appropriate reaction. In addition, the need for autonomy requires that children test the limits imposed on them, which this behavior does.

Needs and coping strategies: Before children are accomplished verbally, yelling and screaming are normal strategies for coping with frustration. As children get older, they become better able to express their disappointment and frustration in words. At this point, recurrent yelling and screaming is more likely to reflect power struggles in the parent-child relationship.

Reinforcement: It's very easy to inadvertently reinforce this kind of behavior by giving in to the child's tantrum and supplying the desired item. Even as a rare event, this response tells the child that by continuing to scream he or she will eventually get what is wanted. If the child sees either parent yell or scream when frustrated or angry, he or she may simply be imitating that behavior.

5. (14.) *Your child screams and yells at his or her sisters and/or brothers.*

Typical Trigger Thoughts

Assumed intent: "You're trying to test me."

Magnification: "This behavior is intolerable."

Labeling: "You're getting out of control"

Alternative Explanations

Temperament: The child's quality of mood, adaptability, sensory threshold, and intensity of reaction are all likely to influence this behavior. A child who is moody and difficult to please and has a hard time coping with disappointment or change will be at increased risk of expressing frustration this way in situations dealing with others. If the child is easily overstimulated and intense in his or her reactions, the risk is even higher.

Developmentally appropriate behaviors: At two years of age, young children have no ability to modulate their reactions to frustration, so this behavior is common. At two-and-a-half, children are characterized by violent, demanding, and bossy behavior. A four-year-old who is provoked is likely to hit, kick, and spit as a typical reaction—and to accompany the action with noise. The need to be best and first that characterizes six-year-olds, and the eight-year-old's insatiable need for mother's attention (which leads to competition with siblings), can both result in levels of frustration that provoke screaming and yelling.

Needs and coping strategies: Until children have developed appropriate verbal skills, screaming and yelling are among the few ways they have available to express intense frustration. This behavior may also be a demand for attention, if the child is feeling unnoticed or unappreciated among his or her siblings. As a consistent problem it may also represent a play for power ("You can't tell me not to yell!").

Reinforcement: Yelling at the child reinforces the notion that yelling is an acceptable way to deal with frustration or to get needs met. It would also reinforce the child whose need was either for attention or to demonstrate power.

6. (16.) *Your child bothers you when you are busy working or talking.*

Typical Trigger Thoughts

Assumed intent: "You're trying to prevent me from getting anything done."

Magnification: "This is intolerable."

Labeling: "You're completely irresponsible."

Alternative Explanations

Temperament: Activity level, tendency to withdraw, distractibility, and persistence may all affect this behavior. Children with a high activity level are inherently noisy and disruptive as they race from one activity to another without ever slowing down. A child who tends to withdraw will be shy and clingy in new situations, which can be disruptive when you're trying to talk to others. In either case, a high level of persistence will exacerbate the problem.

Developmentally appropriate behaviors: Except for when they are around seven years old, children have an almost insatiable need for their parents' attention. It's impossible for them to resist for long the urge to connect with you, even when you are working or talking with someone (especially on the phone). Three-year-olds want to do everything together; five-year-olds want to show you how good they are; eight-year-olds require constant conversation.

Needs and coping strategies: A child who bothers you while you're working or talking may be simply expressing a need for your attention. Since the child's ability to delay gratification is limited, and he or she needs attention *now*, the most direct strategy is to ask for your attention *now*. This strategy works, too, since even an angry response from you fulfills the need. A child who has felt unable to achieve significance in the family through positive contributions will clamor for attention even more than otherwise; the need will seem truly insatiable.

Reinforcement: If your child is expressing a need for attention, then you have probably been reinforcing his or her behavior by responding. Remember, any response, even anger, is attention, and thus reinforces the behavior.

7. (18.) Your child breaks things on purpose.

Typical Trigger Thoughts

Assumed intent: "You're trying to make me mad."

Magnification: "I can't stand it."

Labeling: "You're a spiteful brat."

Alternative Explanations

Temperament: Temperament alone cannot account for this behavior. However, any traits that raise the child's anxiety or frustration would raise the chances of him or her acting out in this way. Difficulty dealing with disappointment, a tendency to become easily overstimulated, high intensity of reaction, negative persistence, and a negative mood would all contribute.

Developmentally appropriate behavior: Children develop independence and autonomy primarily by testing limits and breaking rules. At certain ages, including two-and-a-half and five-and-a-half, the child experiences violent, demanding, explosive emotions. Breaking things can be a way of expressing those emotions and testing limits. But keep in mind that young children learn about the world by interacting with it—by touching, manipulating, bending, twisting, pulling, and hitting things. If something breaks, the child has learned something about it, but the damage may not have been deliberate.

Needs and coping strategies: Your child may deliberately break something in a desperate bid for your attention or in trying to cope with what feels like intolerable frustration. If, however, the behavior seems consistently directed at hurting you, the child's aim is probably revenge. When children perceive that all their attempts to achieve significance in the family have failed or been thwarted, they may see no alternative to striking back.

Reinforcement: If the child's goal is to gain attention, chances are good that any angry response on your part reinforces the behavior—especially in the absence of consistent positive attention. If your child feels so hurt and discouraged in his or her attempts to belong that the only way to gain significance is revenge, you've likely been reacting with anger and outrage. At this point, punishment adds fuel to the anger and reinforces your child's beliefs about the hopelessness of the situation.

8. (19.) Your child doesn't listen to you in public.

Typical Trigger Thoughts

Assumed intent: "You're taking advantage of me."

Magnification: "This is awful."

Labeling: "This is manipulation."

Alternative Explanations

Temperament: A child who is easily distracted will be more likely to tune you out in public or in private. Similarly, a child with a low sensory threshold will be more easily overstimulated in public than at home, and therefore more likely not to hear you because of being bombarded by other stimuli.

Developmentally appropriate behaviors: The development of autonomy and independence is manifested in acts of defiance or opposition. This kind of limit testing is seen at almost every age. At about age seven, children focus inward and become withdrawn; oftentimes they do not even hear their parents talking to them.

Needs and coping strategies: Knowing that your disciplinary responses are likely to be restrained in public, your child may choose to ignore you in those situations as a way of more successfully expressing his or her drive for independence and autonomy. The child may be manifesting the need for power to sustain some sense of significance. In addition, he or she may simply be overstimulated.

Reinforcement: As a result of being limited by the setting, you may not have consistently followed through with disciplinary consequences in response to your child's public misbehavior. If so, your child will have been reinforced to not listen in those situations. If your tendency is to focus on the task at hand when you're in public with your child, you may have unwittingly modeled the problem behavior yourself.

9. (20.) *Your child uses curse words when he or she talks to you.*

Typical Trigger Thoughts

Assumed intent: "You're trying to make me angry."

Magnification: "How dare you talk to me like that."

Labeling: "You're deliberately being a jerk."

Alternative Explanations

Temperament: The traits most likely to affect this behavior are the child's quality of mood, sensory threshold, and intensity of reaction. A child who is hard to please, easily overstimulated, and very intense in his or her reactions is likely to use curse words to emphasize the intensity of his or her feelings.

Developmentally appropriate behaviors: The use of vulgar language and curse words tends to appear around age four, an age characterized by out-of-bounds behavior. At this age, the child enjoys not only the thrill of using forbidden words but the thrill of seeing your (preferably shocked) reaction. Older children, up until about age seven, will use curse words to challenge your authority, as a normal way of developing independence and autonomy.

Needs and coping strategies: Your child may be using curse words as a means of attracting your attention. Cursing may also be an expression of a need to explore new areas of language. If the child perceives no significant place in the family for his or her developing independence, and attempts to gain significance through attention-getting have been thwarted, the child may conclude that he or she can belong only by winning power. The use of forbidden words could be an attempt to gain power.

Reinforcement: If you generally respond angrily to your child's use of curse words, then you've probably been reinforcing the behavior. An attempt to get attention is rewarded even by negative attention, and an attempt to win power is reinforced when you engage in the power struggle. Alternatively, if your child has heard you use curse words in interactions with others, he or she will want to imitate you. Identification with a parent is inherently reinforcing to children.

10. (23.) Your child says things that are not true on purpose.

Typical Trigger Thoughts

Assumed intent: "You're deliberately lying to me."

Magnification: "This behavior is intolerable."

Labeling: "You're so disrespectful."

Alternative Explanations

Temperament: The traits contributing to this behavior are distractibility and level of persistence. A child who has difficulty paying attention or remembering or who tends to daydream, may develop a pattern of making up things. If his or her level of persistence is high, he or she may stick to a story even if it's obviously not true.

Developmentally appropriate behaviors: At around three, children become very absorbed in imaginary play and fantasy, sometimes to the extent of confusing fantasy and reality. Saying things that aren't true can be a manifestation of a healthy fantasy life. This behavior is characteristic of the normal out-of-bounds behavior of four-year-olds. They boast and lie and delight in violating taboos. At six, lying again occurs frequently, as part of a pattern of oppositional behavior.

Needs and coping strategies: Deliberately saying things that are untrue can be a way of coping with feelings of inadequacy. Exaggerating or fabricating certain skills and talents may reflect a need to build self-esteem. Feelings of inadequacy arise when attempts to contribute to the family are neither acknowledged nor validated. Thus this behavior may be a strategy to attract your desperately needed attention. Or, if you and your child have fought over telling the truth, the two of you may be struggling for power over what your child says. Telling a lie can also be a simple attempt to avoid your anger or disappointment.

Reinforcement: If, when a child admits to having misbehaved, you get angry or punish the child, he or she might conclude that telling the truth isn't the best strategy. Lying may be a logical attempt to avoid anger or punishment, and if it's succeessful, that behavior will be reinforced. Furthermore, if your child has ever heard you telling a white lie for convenience's sake, then the fact that he or she is identifying with you reinforces the behavior.

11. (25.) *Your child plays too loudly.*

Typical Trigger Thoughts

Assumed intent: "You're doing it to annoy me."

Magnification: "This is awful."

Labeling: "You're so selfish."

Alternative Explanations

Temperament: Sensory threshold, intensity of reaction, and persistence are the traits most likely to contribute to this behavior. A child who is easily overstimulated, has a forceful, loud response whether happy or unhappy, and who tends to persist in that response, is likely to be a source of this problem behavior.

Developmentally appropriate behaviors: At young ages, children have no ability to modulate their behavior, including their volume. This is particularly true for two-year-olds. For three- to five-year-olds, for whom fantasy play is important, the noises accompanying gun battles, spaceship launches, or movie performances may be excessive. At four, where behavior is characterized by out-of-boundness, playing loudly is especially common.

Needs and coping strategies: When children are tired, hungry, or otherwise stressed, their ability to modulate their volume decreases. Loud behavior may also be a reflection of the child's need for attention. If the behavior occurs in the context of an ongoing struggle with the parent for quieter play, then it problably reflects an attempt to achieve power.

Reinforcement: If you give your child more attention when he or she plays too loudly than when the play is acceptably quiet, then you reinforce the loud behavior. Your child may consistently increase the volume of his or her play until you respond—which also reinforces the loudness. If you try to force the child to play more quietly, you reinforce the power struggle.

12. *(28.) Your child takes things that don't belong to him or her.*

Typical Trigger Thoughts

Assumed intent: "You know better but you're doing it anyway."

Magnification: "You've gone too far this time."

Labeling: "You're getting out of control."

Alternative Explanations

Temperament: Taking things that don't belong to him or her is more likely to reflect a child's needs than any temperamental proclivities. However, certain traits might increase the possibility of such behavior: A tendency to approach new situations (risks) with ease might affect the behavior. And a high level of distractibility (tendency to daydream) might increase the chances of the child taking something without meaning to.

Developmentally appropriate behaviors: Until children are close to five, they basically believe that possession means ownership. Even if they've heard otherwise dozens of times, they don't really understand what it means. Once they get their hands on something, it's theirs. Furthermore, the normal challenges to authority that characterize children's developing independence and autonomy may include breaking the rules about taking things that don't belong to them.

Needs and coping strategies: Your child may take something just to get your attention. Taking things sometimes reflects a powerful unmet need for positive nurturing or attention. If previous attempts to gain attention have been thwarted, the child may resort to gaining significance in the family through winning power. Under these circumstances, taking things that belong to others would reflect an attempt to exert power over your efforts to stop the behavior.

Reinforcement: If your child's behavior is an attempt to attract attention, then even a negative response can reinforce that behavior. If you engage in a power struggle with your child to try to force him or her to stop taking other people's things, you may also inadvertently reinforce the behavior. Finally, your child may be imitating behavior he or she has seen when you take such things as matchbooks from restaurants or toiletries from hotels. The child doesn't see the difference.

13. (29.) *Your child won't answer you when you ask him or her a question.*

Typical Trigger Thoughts

Assumed intent: "You're tuning me out intentionally."

Magnification: "You never listen."

Labeling: "You're a disrespectful brat."

Alternative Explanations

Temperament: The traits most likely to affect this behavior are the child's activity level and distractibility. A child who never slows down is likely to be too busy to answer—or even to hear your question. Similarly, a child who tends to daydream or is forgetful and easily distracted is likely not to hear the question or to get distracted while thinking of an answer.

Developmentally appropriate behaviors: Children's struggle for autonomy involves testing limits; this can include not answering your questions. Especially from about age five, passive defiance of your authority becomes a typical response, with children ignoring you or not responding to you. At around seven years old, children typically become so inwardly focused that at times they might not even hear you.

Needs and coping strategies: This kind of response typically reflects a child's goal of attaining power as a means of achieving significance. "You can't make me answer" is the statement implied by the silence. If the behavior typically occurs when the child is tired, fatigue may be making the child less likely to answer you.

Reinforcement: If you respond to the behavior by getting angry and trying to force your child to answer you, the idea of power as a means of achieving significance will be reinforced. Furthermore, if there are times when you don't answer your child's questions or you respond that way to others, your child's imitation of you will also be a reinforcer.

14. (31.) *Your child demands something immediately.*

Typical Trigger Thoughts

Assumed intent: "You're trying to test me."

Magnification: "I can't stand it."

Labeling: "You're spoiled and selfish."

Alternative Explanations

Temperament: Unpredictable rhythmicity, the child's sensory threshold, and his or her persistence level are the traits most likely to influence this problem. A child who is irregular and unpredictable in his or her patterns of hunger and fatigue will get hungry and tired unexpectedly and demand that those needs be addressed immediately. If the child is easily overstimulated, his or her frustration may feel intolerable. Persistence will increase the child's ability to persevere with his or her demands for immediate gratification.

Developmentally appropriate behaviors: Young children (two to four years old, in particular) have limited ability to delay gratification. When they want something, they want it now. At the same time, they are typically bossy as a way of compensating for their growing sense of their powerlessness in the world.

Needs and coping strategies: The child's immediate demands may in fact be demands for attention. If the child persists in those demands after being told what to expect, it may reflect a quest for power. However, if the child is demanding food, drink, or rest, it might be an appropriate strategy for coping with an essential problem: hunger, thirst, or fatigue.

Reinforcement: If you give in to your child's demands for immediate gratification, you will reinforce that behavior. Perhaps a more important factor is your own strategy of getting your needs met. If you tend to demand that your child meet your needs immediately, he or she might be modeling behavior that you engage in yourself.

15. (33.) *Your child does not share toys.*

Typical Trigger Thoughts

Assumed intent: "You're doing it to annoy me."

Magnification: "This behavior is intolerable."

Labeling: "You're deliberately being selfish."

Alternative Explanations

Temperament: The traits most likely to influence this behavior are quality of mood, tendency toward withdrawal, and adaptability. Moody children who are difficult to please and whose preference in the face of novelty is to keep themselves (and their possessions) to themselves, will have difficulty sharing toys. A difficulty adapting to change or disappointment will exacerbate this problem.

Developmentally appropriate behaviors: This kind of behavior is particularly common in two- to three-year-old children: They simply cannot share. Sharing toys—or anything else—generates too much anxiety. Toward four years old, this possessiveness begins to decrease, but its occasional recurrence is not necessarily developmentally abnormal.

Needs and coping strategies: Refusing to share toys may be the child's attempt to attain power as a means of achieving significance. If the behavior habitually occurs when the child is overstimulated by the environment or the presence of other children, the resistance to sharing could be exacerbated by the situation.

Reinforcement: Trying to force the child to share will result in reinforcing the power struggle. From a different perspective, if the child has been told repeatedly that he or she may not play with your possessions, the behavior may be modeled from you.

16. (34.) *Your child interrupts you when you are talking with someone.*

Typical Trigger Thoughts

Assumed intent: "You're doing it to annoy me."

Magnification: "I hate this."

Labeling: "You are so disrespectful."

Alternative Explanations

Temperament: Adaptability, distractibility, and persistence are the three traits most likely to affect this behavior. A child who has a hard time coping with disappointment or change will have a hard time coping when you shift your attention from him or her and begin talking to someone else. A child who tends to persist in his or her reactions will prolong the pattern of interrupting. And a tendency to forget instructions (such as "Play quietly while I talk") will also exacerbate the problem.

Developmentally appropriate behaviors: Children of all ages need their parents' attention, and this need seems to be especially stimulated when the parent is giving his or her attention to someone else. Young children, in addition, have a complete inability to delay gratification, so when they want your attention, they want it immediately.

Needs and coping strategies: The most likely need being expressed by this behavior is the need for attention. Over time, it may also reflect an attempt to attain power.

Reinforcement: If you continue giving your child attention by scolding him or her for the interruptions or by reminding him or her that you want to finish your discussion, you will reinforce the interrupting. Furthermore, if you interrupt your child when he or she is talking, you will be modeling the problem behavior.

17. (36.) *Your child constantly touches things when you are in a store.*

Typical Trigger Thoughts

Assumed intent: "You're trying to test me."

Magnification: "This is awful."

Labeling: "You're a stubborn, disrespectful brat."

Alternative Explanations

Temperament: Several traits might affect the likelihood of this behavior. If the child has a high activity level and never slows down, he or she may have a hard time containing him- or herself inside a store. A tendency to be overstimulated by sights and sounds will exacerbate this problem. A high level of distractibility will make it more difficult for the child to remember your warnings, while a tendency to approach new situations without fear would make the child less motivated to contain him- or herself.

Developmentally appropriate behaviors: Young children mostly learn about the world through touch. A store is a whole new world, and a child is virtually compelled to touch things, feel them, and pick them up. By age four, the need to learn through touch is greatly reduced. However, it's replaced by the tendency to touch as part of the pattern of out-of-bounds behavior characteristic of this age. Also, touching prohibited articles is a normal developmental strategy for challenging your authority and fostering independence.

Needs and coping strategies: In addition to touching things as a way to learn about them, a child may touch things to attract attention or manifest power. These strategies are usually adopted by children who feel their competence hasn't granted them a significant place in their family.

Reinforcement: If your child's behavior is aimed at attracting attention or demonstrating power, then any response that gives even negative attention or that engages in a power struggle reinforces the behavior. More importantly, your child sees you touching things as you look at labels and prices. He or she imitates your behavior as a way of identifying with you.

18. (39.) Your child screams, yells, and gets in fights during car trips.

Typical Trigger Thoughts

Assumed intent: "You're trying to drive me crazy."

Magnification: "This is intolerable."

Labeling: "You're deliberately being a jerk."

Alternative Explanations

Temperament: Any characteristics that might make it difficult for a child to tolerate the confinements of car travel will increase the likelihood of this behavior; activity level, adaptability, sensory threshold, intensity of reaction, and persistence would all contribute. A child who is typically in constant motion will have a hard time on car trips. This difficulty will be exacerbated if the child adapts poorly to transitions and is easily overstimulated. If in addition, the child is loud and forceful in his or her reactions to frustration and persists in those reactions, then car trips may become intolerable.

Developmentally appropriate behaviors: For very young children, until their developing verbal skills provide an alternative strategy, yelling may be their only means of expressing intense frustration. Even older children have a hard time expressing themselves verbally when their frustration becomes intolerable to them. Children whose struggle for autonomy and separateness from siblings is usually manifested actively will also experience intense difficulties when cooped up in a car.

Needs and coping strategies: Although it's possible that this behavior represents the child's need for attention, or even power, it's more likely to reflect a strategy for coping with frustration. Boredom and fatigue greatly exacerbate this problem.

Reinforcement: Even if the original goal of the behavior wasn't to attract attention, when attention is given as a response, it reinforces the problem behavior.

19. (44.) *Your child doesn't do his or her chores.*

Typical Trigger Thoughts

Assumed intent: "You're defying me."

Magnification: "How dare you do that."

Labeling: "You're so lazy."

Alternative Explanations

Temperament: Activity level, distractibility, and persistence are the three traits most likely to influence this behavior. Children who never slow down, who tend to be easily distracted, or who have difficulty persisting with a task may have a harder time completing chores in a satisfactory way.

Developmentally appropriate behaviors: All children test limits in the service of defining their separateness and independence. Defiance with respect to chores is a typical manifestation of this process. At five years old, defiance is more often seen in dawdling over tasks than in outright refusal to comply. And at seven, the characteristic combination of perseveration and perfectionism may preclude the child's actually completing anything.

Needs and coping strategies: As a reflection of needs, this behavior is likely to indicate the child's strategy for asserting power as a means of achieving significance. If the behavior habitually occurs when the child is tired—for instance at the end of the day or first thing in the morning—fatigue or sleepiness might also contribute to the behavior. In addition, children's capabilities change from year to year. An important factor in this problem is the age-appropriateness of the chore. The child may not be doing his or her chores simply because he or she isn't capable of doing them or doesn't understand what is wanted or expected.

Reinforcement: Engaging in the struggle to force your child to complete his or her chores reinforces the concept that power is the way to achieve significance.

20. (45.) *Your child misbehaves after you have had a bad day.*

Typical Trigger Thoughts

Assumed intent: "You're trying to drive me crazy."

Magnification: "I can't stand this."

Labeling: "You're selfish."

Alternative Explanations

Temperament: Almost any trait when manifested at a difficult level would make this behavior seem more likely, because your own sensitivity to stress is heightened when you've had a bad day. A child with a high activity level will be stressful to deal with at these times, as will a moody child, a clinging child, or one who takes off in pursuit of adventure. Overstimulation, intense reactions, and stubborn persistence further exacerbate the stress level.

Developmentally appropriate behaviors: It's almost inevitable that your child will misbehave when you've had a hard day. At the end of a hard day, your attention is likely to be, not inappropriately, on your own needs. This provides a perfect opportunity for your child—in response to his or her need to develop autonomy—to test the limits. Your focus being elsewhere will also trigger his or her need for attention, which will feel more than usually trying.

Needs and coping strategies: If your hard day has been spent with your child, it's likely he or she is also experiencing some fallout from the day's difficulties. The child may need some positive attention or may feel thwarted by your attempts to cope with the day and need to assert some power. If your day wasn't spent with your child, your tiredness and attempts to protect yourself from further stressful interactions may trigger intense needs for attention in your child.

Reinforcement: If your response to your child's behavior is to attempt to stop the demands for attention or reassert your own power, you're probably reinforcing the behavior. Even negative attention is reinforcing in the absence of positive attention. And engaging in the power struggle is also rewarding because doing so inherently acknowledges your child's power.

Exercise: Understanding Your Child's Behavior

Now that you have read about possible alternative explanations for various problem behaviors, choose the one behavior of your child that you find the most aggravating. Then, using the spaces and steps below, come up with an alternative explanation of the behavior that takes into account your child's temperament, age-apropriate behaviors, needs and coping strategies, and ways in which the behavior may have been reinforced.

Problem behavior:

_____

_____

_____

_____

Alternative Explanations

Temperament: Put a check mark beside each of the traits listed below that may be contributing to this behavior in your child.

_____ Activity level

_____ Quality of mood

_____ Approach/withdrawal

_____ Rhythmicity

_____ Adaptability

_____ Sensory threshold

_____ Intensity of reaction

_____ Distractibility

_____ Persistence

Developmentally appropriate behaviors: Refer back to the descriptions of age-appropriate behaviors on pages 55–85, if necessary. Then make note of which of those behaviors may be contributing to this behavior in your child.

_____

_____

_____

_____

_____

Needs and coping strategies: Put a check mark beside each of the needs or strategies listed below that may be contributing to this behavior in your child.

_____ Belonging

_____ Attention

_____ Power

_____ Revenge

_____ Physical needs (sleep, rest, food, help with something that hurts)

Reinforcement: How might you be reinforcing the misbehavior?

_____

_____

_____

_____

_____

What other factors may be reinforcing the behavior?

_____

_____

_____

_____

_____

5

Changing What You Think

When a parent is stressed, trigger thoughts that magnify, label, or assume intent can start a wildfire. It's like throwing a lit match into a hay field. That's why trigger thoughts can be dangerous deceptions. They distort the situation by making it seem bigger than it is and make your child's behavior seem deliberate and bad.

Trigger thoughts lead you to forget all about the *real* reasons for your child's behavior: his or her temperament, level of development, needs, and the ways the behavior has been reinforced. None of that matters when you've decided that a child is being lazy, willful, spoiled, selfish, or manipulative. And it's impossible to analyze the underlying causes of a child's reactions when you've already concluded that he or she is deliberately trying to annoy you.

Trigger thoughts can leave you feeling helpless. They ignite your anger to a point where all you want to do is shout and blame. But when it quiets down again, nothing has changed. The same conflicts will soon flare up—the same power struggles and the same frustrations. The trigger thoughts and anger haven't fixed anything. They have, in fact, blocked any opportunity for real problem solving.

Three things happen to your child when trigger thoughts and anger prevent you from seeing and addressing the underlying cause of a behavior problem:

- *Your child begins to think of himself or herself as bad.* There's a simple reason for this. "You are bad" is exactly the message that anger conveys, particularly when it is expressed through labeling, magnification, and assumed intent. When your voice is raised, when you are blaming and accusing, your child hears it as a statement about his or her worth. The more frequent your anger, the more entrenched becomes a child's "I'm bad" belief.

- *Your child grows less cooperative.* Young children are usually quite frightened by a parent's anger. It gets their attention, and they often stop the problematic behavior. This tends to reinforce your use of anger, because initially it works so well to solve behavior problems. But if children are the target of frequent anger, they *desensitize*; they become numb. When that happens, parental anger has far less impact than it once did. You have to escalate to higher and higher levels before the child "listens." Chronically angry parents often complain that their kids tune them out, that nothing gets through to them. If people who live near volcanoes get used to the rumbling, is it any wonder that a kid can learn to ignore a parent's rage?

- *Your child becomes alienated and/or angry.* Who wants to be around a person who's angry all the time? You wouldn't. Neither does your child. The numbing process that occurs as a child desensitizes to your anger has far more impact than the conflict situation itself. The child may begin to shut down to you across the board. While retreating from feelings of fear and hurt, he or she may also begin to shut down the sweet, loving feelings, the sense of trust, the joy of being spontaneous and silly. These vulnerable emotions may be replaced by the child's own protective anger or the simple strategy of avoiding you.

How Parents Cope Successfully with Anger

The price of chronic anger is too high; parents realize that and try to cope. Our national survey examined twenty-four specific strategies that parents use to cope with provocative situations. Some are more effective than others. The following is a list of seven coping thoughts that differentiate parents with low anger levels from those with higher anger scores. In other words, these seven coping thoughts were used significantly more often by parents who report less anger.

_____ 1. It's just a stage. Kids have to go through these stages.

_____ 2. This is natural for his or her age.

_____ 3. Don't take it seriously. Keep a sense of humor.

_____ 4. This is just natural impulsiveness.

_____ 5. He or she isn't really trying to do it to me. It's just how he or she is coping right now.

_____ 6. He or she can't help (crying, being angry, interrupting, needing attention, etc.).

_____ 7. Just get through it. You can cope. You don't have to get angry.

These seven thoughts are effective coping strategies which angry parents often forget to use. Notice that thoughts 1, 2, and 4 reframe the behavior as natural and normal for the child's level of development. Number 4 also acknowledges the natural influence of a child's temperament. Thoughts 3 and 7 help you stop magnifying and focus away from trigger thoughts. Number 5 is a reminder that the child's behavior is a way of coping with some underlying need. And thought 6 steers you away from assumed intent, reframing the problem as something the child can't deal with any other way.

Now go back over the list and put a check next to any coping thought that seems true to you or that might help when you're upset. Write the coping thoughts you marked on an index card and tape it to your bathroom mirror. If any of the thoughts you choose doesn't feel quite right to you, modify it any way you prefer. What matters is that it's something you can believe and *use*.

Make it part of your routine to read these coping thoughts *every morning*. The more often you read them, the more likely you will be to use them in provocative situations.

Stopping the Trigger Thoughts

The time to deal with your anger is early rather than late. It's much harder to get control once you start to escalate into a full-fledged argument. As soon as you are aware of irritation, listen to what you're saying to yourself. Notice if you are labeling your child, magnifying the problem, or assuming some obstructive motivation on the part of your child.

When you've identified the trigger thoughts and you can see how you are making yourself angry, there are two ways to stop them. The first is to replace the triggers with a generic coping thought, such as "I'm staying calm. I don't have to get angry. I can cope with this." Anytime you feel irritation starting to rise repeat to yourself the coping thought. Commit yourself right now to using a coping thought each time you notice an angry trigger thought over the next two days.

The second way to stop trigger thoughts is to refute them. Since triggers usually distort reality, your greatest weapon is to talk back with the truth. Get rid of the labels and the exaggeration. Stop assuming negative intent. And remind yourself of other, more realistic ways of viewing the problem.

What follows are examples of how you might talk back to the eighteen trigger thoughts identified in our study (see chapter 3). You'll notice that most of the sample refutations are derived from or combine the seven key coping thoughts described above.

Examples of Talking Back

Trigger Thought	*Realistic View*
Assumed Intent	
1. You're doing it to annoy me.	He isn't really trying to annoy me, it's just how he's coping right now. What does he need?
2. You're defying me.	This is natural impulsiveness; she can't help being angry. What does she really need here?
3. You're trying to drive me crazy.	This is natural; he's trying to cope. He can't help it. He's not doing it *to* me.
4. You're trying to test me (see how far you can go).	Maybe he is, but I can cope; I don't have to get angry. It's natural for his age to test limits.
5. You're tuning me out intentionally.	This is a stage—the "I don't listen" stage. It's natural. Either she can't help it or she's doing it to cope with something.
6. You're taking advantage of me.	It's natural. She wants what she wants and tries to push me to give it to her. This is what kids do! Just keep a sense of humor.
7. You're doing this deliberately (to get back at me, hurt me, spite me, etc.).	He's doing this to cope with *his* feelings and needs. It's not about *me.*
Magnification	
8. I can't stand it.	Kids have to go through these stages. I can cope. I can get through it without blowing up.

Trigger Thought	*Realistic View*
9. This behavior is intolerable.	I don't like it, but I can cope. He can't help doing this; it's how *he* tries to cope. I'm the grownup. I can handle this.
10. You've gone too far this time.	This is just catching me at a bad time. I can deal with it. She isn't trying to do it to me; it's just how she's coping.
11. You never listen.	OK, don't exaggerate. Sometimes he listens, but it's pretty natural for kids to tune out. I need a plan to get his attention without anger.
12. How dare you (look at me like that, talk to me like that, do that, etc.).	I can cope, keep a sense of humor. She's upset and angry. That doesn't mean I have to get angry. Calm down first, then make a plan to deal with this.
13. You turn everything into a (power struggle, fight, lousy time together, nightmare, etc.).	No exaggeration. It isn't always this way. There's something he needs, and this is how he tries to get it. I can cope with this without yelling.

Labeling

14. You're getting out of control.	This is natural impulsiveness. Kids get wild, kids are intense. Forget the labels and calmly set limits.
15. This is manipulation.	Don't take this so seriously. She wants her way, that's natural. Kids are less powerful than adults, so they do what they can to get what they want.

Trigger Thought	*Realistic View*
16. You're so (lazy, malicious, stubborn, disrespectful, ungrateful, willful, selfish, cruel, stupid, bratty, spoiled, contrary, etc.).	Labels make it worse. A lot of this is natural for her age. I can cope and deal with this without blowing up.
17. You're deliberately being mean, a jerk, etc.	No labels. He can't help doing _____ sometimes. That's how he copes with his needs. It's natural and I can handle it calmly.
18. You don't care (what happens, how I feel, who you hurt, etc.).	I don't know how she feels for sure. Labels only make things worse. It's natural for children to focus mostly on themselves.

After reading the examples, you have some ideas about how to talk back to triggers. Right now turn back to chapter 3, and review which of the eighteen trigger thoughts you checked as ones that you use. For each of those triggers, read the sample refutation provided above. Then change or rewrite it so it feels really true and believable to you. Remember, the statements above are only examples. You need to tailor them into effective coping statements that work for *you*. If the example refutation isn't helpful for you, go back to the seven key coping thoughts and see if you get any ideas about how to construct your own more realistic response to the trigger.

For instance, Bill had often used the trigger "You're taking advantage of me." But the sample refutation, "It's natural, he wants what he wants," didn't seem helpful. The truth was that Bill felt pretty unaccepting of his son's behavior. So he looked through the key coping thoughts and finally wrote this refutation: "It's annoying as hell, but I can cope with it. Just because he pushes me doesn't mean I have to blow up. I have to be in charge of my own anger and in charge of the situation." Helen often triggered anger toward her daughter with the thought "You never listen." But the sample refutation, which suggested not exaggerating and that it's natural for kids to tune out, was more annoying than helpful. Helen decided to talk back to her trigger in the following way: "She listens when I clearly tell her the consequences of ignoring me. It's *my* responsibility to do that."

Coping with Unexpected Trigger Thoughts

For our study, we identified some of the most common, and damaging, trigger thoughts parents use. But those aren't the only thoughts parents have that can cause a rage to flare up in interactions with a child. When you run into a trigger thought you aren't prepared for, you need to develop your own method for talking back. Here are four steps you can take for turning a trigger thought into a realistic response to your child's problem behavior.

1. Assess the Real Cause of the Behavior.

Use the skills you learned in chapter 4 to identify the role of the child's temperament, developmental level, his or her underlying needs, and reinforcers in your child's responses.

2. Realistically Assess the Size of the Problem.

Don't magnify. Avoid thinking such things as "This is outrageous . . . ridiculous behavior . . . totally out of control . . . can't stand it." Replace exaggerations with accurate, behavioral descriptions of *exactly* what's happening: "Bill has been running through the house making loud war whoops for the past five minutes." Notice that the behavioral description focuses on Bill's actual behavior and how long he has been doing it—no inflammatory excess, no hyperbole. Just a straight, clear description of what's happening. "Saundra turned an eight-foot strip of the lawn into mud by wetting it down and sliding on it." Notice the careful avoidance of exaggeration. There are no magnifying trigger thoughts like "This is totally thoughtless. The lawn is completely destroyed. There's absolutely no concern here for anybody else."

It may seem strange to think about problem behavior in terms of facts only and to confine yourself to thoughts that feel stiff and passionless. But exaggeration only makes you angrier, less in control, and ultimately less likely to find real solutions to the problem.

3. Replace Negative Labels with Neutral Descriptions.

This is really an elaboration of step 2. Terms like *crazy, lazy, stupid, cruel, spoiled,* and so forth make you see red. Trigger thoughts that use these labels are so provocative that you can quickly escalate to a shouting rage. Drop labeling in favor of a clear, accurate description of what's happening.

Of course, this doesn't feel nearly as satisfying as shouting some epithet. And it's work to get into that "just the facts" mindset. But cutting out the global labels really helps with anger. If you have trouble remembering to do it, learn to ask yourself this simple question when you're starting to get mad: "What *exactly* is happening here?" When Rene is late getting home from school for the third time in a week, ask "What *exactly* is happening here?" Then answer with just the facts. And if you don't have all the facts, ask her for more information. The process will go very differently than if you labeled her as stubborn, willful, and bratty. Likewise, when Zack has pulled the laundry off the line and dragged it over some boxes and lawn chairs: "It's a fort," he says. But you see muddy footprints on the sheets and towels. What is a clear, accurate description of what's happening here? As you steer away from labels, you'll find your anger far easier to control.

4. Remind Yourself That You Can Cope and Keep Your Cool.

It's crucial to affirm that you will stay calm and cope—without anger.

New Uses for Your Anger Diary

It's time to get some practice coping with your trigger thoughts. You'll need to get back to your anger diary, but now you'll set it up a little differently. Here's the new format (a form which you can photocopy is included at the end of this chapter):

Date	Situation	Trigger Thoughts	Anger Felt	Realistic View	Anger Felt

For the next two weeks, record every anger episode with your kids in the Situation column. Note your trigger thoughts and rate how angry (on a scale of 1 to 10) they make you feel *right now*. Next, use the preceding four steps to respond to the triggers in the Realistic View column. Then rate your anger again and notice whether it has decreased.

Example

Here are four entries from Richard's diary. You'll see shortly how he developed his refutations for the Realistic View column.

Date	Situation	Trigger Thoughts	Anger Felt	Realistic View	Anger Felt
6/7	Rebecca put her pet rat in the refrigerator.	This is stupid, cruel behavior. She's incapable of caring for an animal.	5	I can handle this calmly. She put the rat in the refrigerator because she thought it was a good place to climb around in. This is normal, I guess, for a seven-year-old. She had no idea how it would affect the rat.	2

6/7	Rebecca said, "I don't have to. I'm my own boss," when I asked her to bring her laundry down from her room.	She's defying me. She's trying to control me and everything else in this house.	6	I notice when she does this, she gets a lot of attention. I guess we're reinforcing it. She's being assertive about her opinions; she simply doesn't want to bring the laundry down. I can calmly find a way to reinforce her to help me.	1
6/8	Rebecca kept interrupting with loud singing or top-of-her-voice chanting while I was working on my sales reports.	She's trying to keep me from getting my work done. She never listens when I tell her to cool it and be quiet.	4	She listens to me for a moment, and then forgets. She's a loud, exuberant kid. That's just her. And she probably needs some attention right now. Relax and stay calm.	1
6/9	Rebecca hid under her bed when it was time to go to school. I called and looked all over the house for her.	This is outrageous, willful crap. I can't stand it. This is nuts. She's deliberately making us late.	7	Calm down. You can deal with this. She just hides because it's fun. Don't take it so seriously. It's natural at her age to be silly. It's not a huge deal, even if we are late. I'll tell her she doesn't get to play at Gina's house after school if she doesn't come now.	2

Notice that in the first entry, Richard starts by reminding himself that he can cope. Then he describes the facts—exactly how Rebecca explained her behavior. When Richard tries to realistically understand Rebecca's behavior, he realizes that this is normal for her age level. He's careful to delete labels like *stupid*, *cruel*, and *incapable of caring*.

In the second entry, Richard sees that he's assuming intent. Then he looks for realistic explanations for Rebecca's refusal to get the laundry. Temperament, level of development, and underlying needs didn't seem to explain Rebecca's noncooperation. After some careful thought, Richard begins to see how the negative attention Rebecca gets might be reinforcing her behavior. Richard then replaces phrases like "She's defying me" with a simple description of her behavior—being assertive about her needs and wants. Finally, Richard decides to develop an effective reinforcement for cooperative behavior.

In the third entry, Richard begins by more realistically describing the situation and correcting his exaggeration. In response to his assumed-intent trigger, Richard does some thinking about Rebecca's temperament: "She's a loud, exuberant kid. That's just her." That thought feels a lot better than imagining that she was trying deliberately to upset him. Finally, Richard reminds himself to handle the situation calmly.

The fourth entry finds Richard coping with labeling, magnification, and assumed intent simultaneously. He reminds himself to stay calm, then reframes Rebecca's behavior as an attempt to have fun—a more accurate assessment. Rebecca's hiding didn't seem related to underlying needs or temperament. As Richard thinks more about it, the behavior seems normal for her age. His job is to figure out a reinforcement that will get her to cooperate.

On the next page is a blank anger diary form. You can photocopy it and use it for your entries during the next two weeks. Try to fill in the Realistic View column on the same day that each incident occurs. And don't forget to fill out the anger ratings to see whether talking back makes you feel less upset.

Date	Situation	Trigger Thoughts	Anger Felt	Realistic View	Anger Felt

6

Changing What You Do

Anger is mostly a cognitive problem. In the last chapter, you learned to control anger by controlling what you think about a provocative situation. But sometimes—when oatmeal is dripping from the ceiling or you find a flaming potholder in the toaster—it's hard to concentrate on positive thinking. You are seized by an overwhelming urge to *do something*.

This chapter is about changing what you do. Our study showed that there are four behavioral coping mechanisms that parents consistently and successfully use in anger-provoking situations. Two are self-management skills: relaxation and identifying what your child really needs. They are covered in this chapter. The other two are assertive communication skills; they are covered in chapter 7.

Relaxation

There are three parts to using relaxation to fight anger:

- Learn to relax your body on a regular schedule so that the cumulative stresses of family life don't affect you so strongly.

- Tune into your body to recognize early warning signals, so you can stop anger before it starts.

- Pause and breathe before responding to provocative situations.

Three Weeks to Relaxation

Stress has been called the fuel of anger. It accumulates continuously, so you need to relax and relieve stress every day to get good results. Set aside one or two times each day when you can be alone in a quiet place to practice your relaxation exercises. If you can't find a regular time to relax every day, that alone could be a major factor in your stress and irritability—your anger fuel tank is always full.

Since the instructions for these techniques are detailed, and most of the exercises are more effective if you do them with your eyes closed, it's a great help to tape-record the instructions. Read them slowly and clearly into the microphone, with appropriate pauses where needed.

Week One: Deep Breathing and Progressive Muscle Relaxation

Full, natural breathing is an antidote to stress. The first thing that happens when you experience a stressful situation is that you hold your breath or start taking short, shallow breaths. Practicing deep breathing every day for a week will relax you and teach you to pay attention to your breathing. This technique and those that follow have been adapted from the *Relaxation & Stress Reduction Workbook* (Davis, Eshelman, and McKay 1994).

1. Lie down on your back with your arms and legs uncrossed. Close your eyes. Try to consciously let go of any tension you sense in your body. Wriggle around until you are comfortable.

2. Place one hand on your belly and the other on your chest.

3. Inhale slowly and deeply, through your nose if you can. Fill your abdomen, raising the hand on your belly. Push the air into your belly. Your belly should rise a lot, and the hand on your chest should move only a little and only with your belly.

4. Exhale through your mouth, making a gentle "whooshing" noise. Keep your mouth, tongue, and jaw relaxed as you gently blow out. If you experience difficulty breathing into your abdomen, press your hand down on your belly as you exhale and let your abdomen push your hand back up as you inhale deeply. An alternative is to lie on your stomach and take deep breaths so you can feel your abdomen pushing against the floor.

5. Continue to take long, slow, deep breaths into your belly and let them out gently. Focus on the sound and the movement of your belly. You will become more and more relaxed.

6. Do this exercise for at least 5 minutes; 10 or 15 minutes of practice is even better. At the end of the exercise, scan your body for tension, and notice how much more relaxed you are than when you started. This is how you should breathe during all the relaxation exercises that follow.

The progressive muscle relaxation technique works directly on tense muscles: you progressively clench and release all the major muscle groups in your body.

1. Lie down on your back in a comfortable position. Start by clenching your right fist, very tightly, studying the tension you create. Keep it clenched for about 7 seconds, really noticing the tension. Then relax. Feel the looseness in your right hand and notice how it contrasts with the tension. Repeat this again with the same fist, clenching for 7 seconds and releasing. Repeat the whole sequence with your left fist. Then repeat the sequence with both fists at once.

2. Now bend your elbows and clench your biceps in a "body-builder" pose. Keep your biceps as tight as you can for 7 seconds, then release them. Feel relaxation flood your biceps. Feel the difference. Repeat at least once.

3. Wrinkle your forehead as tight as you can for 7 seconds, and then release the tension. Feel your forehead smooth out and notice the contrast. Now frown again and notice the strain as it spreads. Hold the tension for 7 seconds, and then relax. Next, close your eyes as tight as you can for 7 seconds. Relax and let your eyes return to being gently closed. Feel the difference. Bite down gently and clench your jaw (skip this step if you have chronic pain from a temporomandibular joint dysfunction). Notice how tension spreads out from your jaw muscles. Relax and let your mouth hang open a little. Appreciate the contrast between tension and relaxation. Next, press your tongue against the roof of your mouth, really hard. Feel the tension in the back of your mouth. Relax. Purse your lips into an O shape and compress them hard. Relax with an exhale and make a rude blubbery sound with your lips, like a horse. Notice how relaxed you have made your forehead, eyes, jaw, mouth, tongue, and lips. Repeat this entire step once.

4. Press your head backwards and notice the tension in your neck. Roll your head to each side and see how the stress changes location. Then bring your head forward, trying to press your chin to your chest. Feel the tension in your throat and neck. Relax, letting your head fall back gently. Notice the relaxation spreading through your neck and throat, moving into your shoulders and back. Next shrug your shoulders, hunching your head down. Try to stuff your shoulders into your ears, and hold the tension for 7 seconds. Relax and feel the comfort flood your shoulders, warm and heavy. Repeat once.

5. Now breathe in and fill your lungs completely, building tension in your chest. Hold your breath for 7 seconds, and

then exhale with a hissing sound, relaxing your chest entirely. Breathe in and out this way several times, sinking deeper into relaxation with each exhalation. Then tighten your stomach and hold it in for 7 seconds. Focus on the tension, then release and focus on the relaxation. Place your hand on your stomach and try breathing air into your stomach, tensing it. Then exhale and relax. Next, try arching your back as much as you can without pain and without tension in the rest of your body. Hold for 7 seconds, and then relax. Repeat this entire step. Then rest quietly for a moment, savoring the relaxation.

6. Press down on your heels to flex your thighs and buttocks. Hold the tension for 7 seconds, and then release. Concentrate on the difference between relaxation and tension. Next, curl your toes downward to make your calves tight. Hold and release. Pull your toes up towards your head, putting tension into your shins. Hold and relax. Repeat this step once.

7. Lie completely still, heavy and warm, scanning your body slowly from feet to head, noticing the relaxation in every muscle of your body.

Progressive muscle relaxation is the best way to learn how to completely relax your body. At first it will be time consuming, as you concentrate on each small muscle group and do all the required repetitions. But after you have learned what relaxed muscles feel like and you can quickly create and release tension in your body, you can use this shorthand procedure:

1. Clench both fists and bend both elbows in a bodybuilder pose, hold for 4 seconds, and relax.

2. Push your head back, roll it in a complete circle while frowning, clenching your jaw, pursing your lips, and pushing your tongue against your palate. Roll your head for 4 seconds, and release.

3. Inhale deeply into your chest, arching your back. Hold 4 seconds, then exhale and relax. Inhale deeply into your stomach, tensing it for 4 seconds. Then exhale and relax.

4. Pull your toes back toward your face. Hold for 4 seconds, and then release. Curl your toes, and tighten your calves, thighs, and buttocks. Hold the tension for 4 seconds, and then release.

Week Two: Relaxation Without Tension

After a week of feeling the difference between tensing and relaxing each muscle group, you can switch to relaxation without tension. This cuts out the tensing part of each step of progressive muscle relaxation, cutting the time required by half. You can become completely relaxed in only 5 to 7 minutes.

With practice, you'll be able to relax each muscle group using mental focus alone, without needing to first tense each muscle group. If you have difficulty sensing the difference between tensed and relaxed muscles in your body, continue to use the Week One instructions until you can easily feel the difference.

1. Sit in a comfortable chair with arms that support your arms. Move around a little to get comfortable.

2. Start by focusing on your breathing. Inhale deeply and feel the air first filling your stomach, then your lower chest, finally your upper chest. Hold your breath a moment, sitting up straighter in the chair. Then exhale slowly through your mouth, releasing all tension and worry with the escaping air. At the end of the exhalation, relax your stomach and chest and slump slightly in the chair. Continue to take long, slow breaths, becoming more and more relaxed with each one.

3. Relax your forehead, smoothing out all the lines. Keep breathing deeply. Now relax your eyebrows. Just let all the tension melt away. Let the relaxation spread to your jaw. Let your lips part and your tongue relax. Let all tension go. Continue breathing in and out slowly. Feel the air relax your throat. Notice that your entire face feels peaceful and calm.

4. Roll your head gently and feel your neck relax. Release your shoulders. Let them drop all the way down. Your

neck is loose, and your shoulders are heavy and hanging low. Now let the relaxation travel down through your arms, relaxing your biceps and triceps, your forearms, and finally your hands and fingers. Your arms are warm and heavy and loose. Feel the relaxation that extends from the top of your head downward through your shoulders and arms.

5. Now focus on your stomach and chest. Breathe in deeply and hold your breath to expand your entire torso. Let the breath out slowly through your mouth in a smooth stream.

6. Notice relaxation moving into your abdomen. Feel all the muscles there release their tension as your abdomen assumes its natural shape. Relax your waist and back. Continue to breathe deeply. Notice how loose and heavy the upper half of your body has become.

7. Now relax the lower half of your body. Feel your buttocks sink into the chair. Relax your thighs. Relax your knees. Feel the relaxation travel though your calves to your ankles, through your feet to your toes. Your feet feel warm and heavy, resting solidly on the floor. Feel the relaxation deepen with each breath.

8. Continue to breathe deeply and scan your body for tension. Your legs are relaxed. Your back is relaxed. Your shoulders and arms are relaxed. Your face is relaxed. You feel calm, peaceful, warm, and relaxed.

9. If any muscle group felt difficult to relax, return your attention to it now. Is your back still a little tight? Your shoulders? Your forehead? Your jaw? Tune into the muscles and tense them a little. Hold the tension, then release it. Feel these last tight muscles go slack and join the rest of your body in complete relaxation.

Although these instructions are shorter and seem simpler than progressive muscle relaxation, the skill level required is actually higher. Make sure that you are draining all the tension from each muscle group and that tension is not creeping back in when you turn your attention to a new group. After 5 to 7 minutes of relaxation without tension, you should feel just as relaxed as you did in your first week of progressive muscle relaxation.

Week Three: Cue-Controlled Relaxation

Cue-controlled relaxation reduces the time you need to relax to 2 or 3 minutes. You focus on your breathing and train yourself to relax exactly when you tell yourself to. Through repetition, you form an association between the mental command "Relax" and true muscle relaxation.

Before trying this method, be sure you are comfortable with the relaxation without tension procedure you practiced in Week Two. This technique is much easier to learn if you make yourself a tape of the instructions.

1. Make yourself comfortable in your chair, with your arms at your sides and your feet flat on the floor. Keep your eyes open. Take a deep breath and hold it for a moment. Let it out in a slow steady stream, blowing away the worries of the day and your hassles with your kids—far, far away. Empty your lungs completely and feel your stomach and chest relax.

2. Now take about 30 seconds to relax your whole body, from your forehead all the way down to your toes, using the relaxation without tension method. If you need more time, that's fine. (*When making your tape, pause for 30 seconds here.*)

3. You feel peaceful and at ease. Your stomach and chest are moving in an out with slow, even breaths. With each breath, the feeling of relaxation deepens.

4. Continue to breathe deeply and regularly, silently saying "Breathe in" to yourself as you inhale and "Relax" as you exhale. (*When making your tape, allow about 8 seconds for each repetition.*)

   Breathe in . . . Relax . . .

   Breathe in . . . Relax . . .

Breathe in . . . Relax . . .

Breathe in . . . Relax . . .

Breathe in . . . Relax . . .

Feel each breath bring peace and calm in and float worry and tension out.

5. Continue to breathe this way for several minutes, saying "Breathe in . . . Relax . . ." to yourself silently. *(When making your tape, leave a couple of minutes of silence here. This part works best when you say the words to yourself silently.)* Focus all your attention on the words in your head and on the process of breathing. Feel *all* your muscles relax more and more deeply with each breath. Let the word "Relax" crowd every other thought from your mind. Close your eyes to deepen your focus.

6. Listen to the words again as you continue to breathe in . . . and relax.

   Breathe in . . . Relax . . .

   Breathe in . . . Relax . . .

   Breathe in . . . Relax . . .

   Breathe in . . . Relax . . .

   Breathe in . . . Relax . . .

7. Continue to breathe, saying these words in your head, for a few minutes. Feel each inhalation bring peace and calm in and each exhalation float worry and tension out. *(Stop recording your tape here.)*

8. If you have time, repeat the entire procedure after a recovery period of 10 to 15 minutes.

After you've practiced cue-controlled relaxation for a week or so, you have begun to learn how calm and peaceful it can help you feel. Continue to set aside time to do your cue-controlled relaxation sequence *daily*. Another option would be the breath-counting meditation described next. The point is to commit yourself to the daily discipline of a relaxation exercise.

The cue phrase "Breathe in . . . Relax" is something you should use in any anger-provoking situation. While saying to yourself "Breathe in . . . Relax," try to release muscle tension throughout your body.

Breath-Counting Meditation

If you liked the process of learning cue-controlled relaxation, you may want to explore deeper levels of relaxation by moving on to a similar exercise that has been part of eastern spiritual practice for centuries, breath-counting meditation. This is optional in terms of the anger-control training presented in this book, but it gives you a classical meditation technique that you can continue to practice.

1. Sit or lie down, and get comfortable. Take several deep breaths. Either close your eyes or fix them on a spot about four feet in front of you. Your eyes may or may not be focused.

2. Take deep but not forced belly breaths. As you do, focus your attention on each part of the breath: the inhalation, the turn (the point at which you stop inhaling and start exhaling), the exhalation, the pause (between exhaling and inhaling), the turn (the point at which you start to inhale), the inhalation, and so on. Pay careful attention to the pause. What are the sensations in your body as you pause between breaths?

3. As you exhale, say "one." Count the next exhalation as "two," the next as "three," and the next as "four." Then begin again with "one." If you lose count, simply start over with "one."

4. When you discover that your mind has wandered away from the counting into thought, note it; then gently return to the counting of your breaths. It is inevitable that your mind will wander. The essence of meditation is noticing

that it has wandered and returning it to the object of focus, in this case, your breathing.

5. If a particular sensation in your body catches your attention, such as an itch or a pain, focus on the sensation until it recedes. Then return your attention to inhaling, exhaling, and counting.

If you wish, you can try the following variation: Begin by counting your breaths for several minutes. Then stop the actual counting and give your attention to the sensations of breathing. Focus on your abdomen as it expands and contracts. Can you sense how the size of the empty space in your abdomen grows and shrinks as your breath goes in and out of your belly? At first, you may have more thoughts when you practice this way than you had when you were counting breaths. The counting keeps your mind returning in a small circle of numbers, which leaves less room for rising thoughts. Do not be disturbed by your mind's wandering. Simply note each thought and then return your awareness to the sensations of your breath. Every now and then, you may come across a thought that you find enticing and want to contemplate. Tell yourself you will consider this thought when the meditation period is over and let it go. The sounds of the outside world will cross and recross the boundaries of your awareness. Note their passing and return to your breathing.

Tuning Into Early Warning Signs

The early warning signs of anger are certain physical symptoms that everybody experiences just before anger hits. Think about the last time you got angry—actually close your eyes and try to reexperience the events that led up to getting angry. Pay attention to what was going on in your body.

Like all strong emotions, anger causes a complex physiological arousal that affects your entire body. Here are just some of the physical sensations that can be early warning signs of anger:

Faster heart rate

Stronger heartbeat

Heavy breathing

Rapid breathing

Shortness of breath

Feeling hot

Flushed skin

Sweatiness

Butterflies in stomach

Tightness in chest or stomach

Tense muscles in neck, shoulders, arms, fists

Grinding jaw

Narrowed eyes

Light seems brighter or dimmer

Tunnel vision

Noises seem louder or softer

Dizziness

The next time you get angry, notice which of these symptoms you feel *early* in the anger reaction. Those symptoms are your early warning signs. As soon as you notice them, it's a signal to practice deep breathing and cue-controlled relaxation to stop your anger.

Jake was a house painter who took good care of his expensive brushes. One afternoon he awoke from a nap and wandered out onto the patio, where his four-year-old son, Arthur, was "painting" with apple juice and Dad's favorite brush. As Jake watched Arthur grind the sticky brush into the dirty cement floor, Jake felt his gut clench deep inside him and his face get hot.

These were his early warning signs. They told him to immediately turn away, breathe deeply, and tell himself "Breathe in . . . Relax" before saying anything to Arthur. Paying attention to these early warning signs saved Jake from yelling at his happily occupied son and scaring him. Jake was able to gently rescue his favorite brush and replace it with an old brush that was already ruined. "Here," he said, "this brush is for kids—you can keep it for your own."

Pause and Breathe—Mini Time-Outs for Parents

This is a technique that allows you to handle anger-provoking situations by shutting your mouth, stopping your thoughts, and opening your lungs. As soon as you notice the early warning signs, take the following steps:

1. Talk back using brief coping thoughts. Say to yourself, strongly and assertively, "Relax now. You can cope. You can stay calm." Put these statements in your own words. Experiment until you find the phrasing that is easiest for you to remember and most effective in reminding you to relax. Here are some examples of useful coping thoughts that you can say to yourself:

   No anger, no yelling.

   Stop! Freeze! Think this out.

   Calm, peace, and reason.

   Time to calm down.

2. Switch all your attention to your breathing. Cue deep breathing by saying to yourself "Breathe in ... Relax." Take long, slow breaths, inhaling through your nose and exhaling through your mouth, just as you did in the deep breathing exercise. You don't have to lie down on the floor, but you can put your hand on your belly as a reminder to take deep, natural breaths.

3. If you can, it will help to physically turn away from the scene. Just turn your back on your daughter jumping up and down on the new couch or turn away from your son

and the video game he refuses to turn off. The simple act of turning aside or turning your back puts distance between you and your child. It's like a brief time-out in which you can remove yourself ever so slightly from the situation and calm down.

4. If you are really getting steamed, it's not a bad idea to increase the separation and actually take a "parental time-out." Leave the room and take the time you need to calm down, get perspective on the situation, and figure out a constructive response.

This simple behavioral coping technique does three things:

- It stops whatever anger-producing thoughts you might have been having and focuses your thinking on the relaxation process.

- It stops the stress reaction by slowing and deepening your breathing. It is literally impossible to be in a rage and to take long, slow breaths at the same time.

- It buys you time to figure out what to say and do. This is no more than Grandma's classic advice to count to ten, but it works wonders.

What Your Child Really Needs

Instead of getting suckered into the same old losing battles, you can sometimes outflank anger by providing what your child *really* needs in a situation.

Figuring out what your child really needs is what you can think about after you tell yourself "No anger, stay calm" to clear away angry thoughts. As you learned to do in chapter 4, ask yourself what your child's behavior means.

Is your son's rude language a bid for attention from you or other kids? Is your daughter showing off to get some praise? Is your son trying to get something from you that he doesn't know how to ask for directly? Maybe he is unsure about what he can get away with in the store or the car and is testing the limits.

Is there some need your child doesn't even recognize that you can figure out? For instance, maybe your daughter is just tired or hungry and it's coming out as whining and clinging. Is there something your little boy is trying to tell you by refusing to go to sleep? For example, maybe he's afraid of the dark and you should just leave the light on. Maybe he just needs a hug and a kiss or a quick story to take his mind off school the next day.

Figuring out what your child might be needing often requires that you put yourself in your child's place. Try to empathize, to feel what it's like to be three or five or nine years old. Imagine what it's like to be small and weak, to be unable to communicate clearly, to be ignorant of a lot of vocabulary and social conventions that adults take for granted. Imagine being entirely dependent on huge, mysterious adults for everything you need.

Once you have an inkling of what your child might really need, provide it and see what happens. You can't really go wrong. At best, you will distract yourself from anger and fill your child's need, ending the conflict. At worst, you will guess wrong and have to guess again, but at least you will have avoided an upset.

To get practice in quickly identifying a child's hidden needs, here's a checklist of things that kids frequently need. Make half a dozen copies of the checklist. Then think back to the last six anger episodes in your family. For each situation, check the possible needs that you could have filled instead of getting angry, and write a brief plan for coping that you can use in similar situations in the future.

Situation: _____

_____

_____

_____

	Possible Need	**Coping Plan**
_____	Food	
_____	Water	
_____	Rest	
_____	Time to calm down	
_____	Sleep	
_____	Safety, security	
_____	Attention	
_____	Hugs, kisses	
_____	Praise	
_____	Diversion, distraction	
_____	Help doing things	
_____	Help solving a problem	
_____	To be listened to	
_____	Freedom, autonomy, power	
_____	Clear limits and rules	
_____	Consistency	
_____	Stimulation, activity	
_____	_____	
_____	_____	

Example

Here is an example of how Jane used this checklist to figure out a coping plan for car trips with her three-year-old and five-year-old daughters.

Situation: Driving to Grandma's, 3 hours in the car, kids whining and fighting with each other. Yelling at them to leave each other alone.

Possible Need	Coping Plan
_X_ Food	Take lots of snacks, fruit
_X_ Water	Take fruit juice
_X_ Rest	Plan more stops
___ Time to calm down	
_X_ Sleep	Put the younger one up front to nap
___ Safety, security	
___ Attention	
___ Hugs, kisses	
_X_ Praise	Notice when they do well
_X_ Diversion, distraction	Get more kids' tapes and games for the car
___ Help doing things	
___ Help solving problems	
___ To be listened to	
___ Freedom, autonomy, power	
_X_ Clear limits and rules	Seatbelts on, no hitting
___ Consistency	

___X___ Stimulation, activity   Races during stops, frisbee

____ _____

____ _____

Special Considerations—What Not to Do

One behavior that will consistently make an anger problem worse is drinking alcohol or taking drugs. It only takes one or two drinks to make the average person more irritable with children. Even if you're usually a cheerful drinker around your kids, alcohol lowers your inhibitions and impairs your judgment. When a very provocative situation arises, you will be more prone to anger and making mistakes. The withdrawal/hangover phase following alcohol or drug intake is also another time when you will be more irritable.

7

Changing What You Say

This chapter is about replacing angry communication with assertive communication. Angry communication is usually ineffective. You may get your child's attention, but nothing really changes. The old problem behaviors keep showing up again and again.

Why Anger Doesn't Work

Your main goal as a parent is to raise your child to be a mature, responsible adult. That means your child has to learn to make choices about his or her behavior and to take responsibility for the consequences of those choices. Your anger won't help a child to make responsible choices. In fact, it will interfere with that learning, for the following reasons:

- Your anger—a shout no less than a slap—is punishing to your child. Punishment doesn't teach a child responsibility—mostly he or she learns to avoid getting caught. If you yell at your child when you catch him or her stealing cookies from the cookie jar, the child might realize the yelling can be avoided by not stealing cookies. But the only certain lesson is "I can avoid the yelling by not getting *caught* stealing cookies."

- Your anger is frightening to your child. Your child already knows that you're bigger and stronger and could do something that would really hurt. When you're angry, you are loud and seemingly out of control—and therefore more frightening. It's impossible to learn much when you're frightened.

- Your anger often triggers anger in your child—and the desire for revenge. In order to learn responsibility, your child has to make the connection between what he or she did and why that behavior isn't acceptable. When your child is angry or consumed with fantasies of revenge, those thoughts are going to interfere with any learning about responsibility. This fact—that anger begets anger—leads in many families to an ever-increasing spiral of punishment and revenge.

But if anger isn't the answer, then what is?

Assertive Communication with Your Child

Your kids aren't necessarily going to do what you want. However, if children don't *know* what you want, the chances they'll do it are remote. Children, for the most part, do want their parents to be happy. So knowing clearly what a parent wants can increase the child's motivation for complying. The purpose of assertive communication is to give your child clear, specific information about your expectations. There are three parts to an assertive message: (1) your feelings about (or reactions to) your child's behavior, (2) why his or her behavior affects you in this way, and (3) what you want to change.

Identifying Your Feelings

The first step in assertive communication is to identify feelings *other than anger* elicited by your child's behavior. When Emily pulled her hand away from her father as they were crossing the street, her father was terrified. When Rickie had a tantrum in the supermarket, his mother felt embarrassed and helpless. And when Kai left the kitchen a mess, his mother felt frustrated. In the spaces below, write brief descriptions of three incidents where your child misbehaved, and next to each write a feeling other than anger that you felt at the time. If you have trouble identifying a specific feeling, use the following list as a guide (but don't be limited by it):

anxious	embarrassed	sad
apprehensive	exasperated	terrified
concerned	frightened	threatened
confused	frustrated	unappreciated
disappointed	helpless	upset
discouraged	resentful	uptight

What I Feel

Situation 1: _____

What I Felt: _____

Situation 2: _____

What I Felt: _____

Situation 3: _____

What I Felt: _____

Understanding Your Feelings

The next step is to identify why your child's behavior affects you the way it does. Why do you feel anxious, disappointed, resentful, or threatened? Emily's father felt terrified because he thought Emily might get hit by a car. Rickie's mother was embarrassed by his tantrum because she thought that it reflected badly on her skills as a parent and that she would be judged by the other customers. She felt helpless because her skills in reasoning with her son didn't work. And Kai's mother was frustrated at the mess in the kitchen because she was tired and had to clean it up before she could prepare dinner.

Review the three situations you described above and the feelings you felt in each instance. Then in the space below write a brief explanation of why your child's behavior affected you in that way, why you felt the way you did in response to the behavior.

Why I Feel This Way

Situation 1: _____

_____

Situation 2: _____

_____

Situation 3: _____

_____

Determining What You Want

The third step is to describe what you want from your child in the particular situation. Be as clear and specific as possible. "I want you to do what I tell you to" is too vague to be valuable. Even "I want you to clean your room" could be more specific; for instance, "I want you to pick your clothes up off the floor and either hang them in your closet or put them in the dirty clothes hamper; take the dirty dishes into the kitchen and put them in the sink; and put your toys and books away in their shelves." The clearer and more specific you can be, the less room there is for ambiguity and misunderstanding.

Emily's father could say to Emily, "I want you to hold my hand all the way across the street." Rickie's mother might tell him, "I would like you to tell me in words how disappointed you are when I won't buy candy." And Kai's mother could say to Kai, "After you make yourself a snack, I want you to put away the food and put the dirty dishes in the dishwasher. And then please sponge down the counters."

In the spaces below, write a statement describing what you want from your child in each of the three situations you listed above. Make your statements as clear and specific as possible.

What I Want

Situation 1: _____

_____

Situation 2: _____

_____

Situation 3: _____

_____

Completing the Assertive Message

Putting together these three components—your feelings, why you have those feelings, and what you want—provides your child with all the information he or she needs to make a choice about how to behave. (Remember: Kids won't necessarily behave the way you want, but at least they'll have the information to make such a choice.)

Here's the generic formula for a complete assertive message: "When you _____ (description of the behavior), I feel _____ because _____. I want/would like you to _____. Note that the effectiveness of assertive communication lies in the fact that it doesn't attack or criticize the child. The "you are bad" message that anger conveys is replaced by a clear statement about your feelings and expectations.

Emily's father's assertive statement might look like this: "When you pull away from me in the middle of the street I'm terrified because you might get hit by a car. I want you to hold my hand all the way across."

For Rickie's mother, the statement might look like this: "When you have a tantrum in the store if I won't buy you candy, I get embarrassed. I worry that people will think I haven't taught my son how to behave well. And I feel helpless because I can't talk to you when you're in that state. I would like you to tell me in words how disappointed you are."

And for Kai's mother, the statement might be this: "When you leave the kitchen a mess I feel frustrated because I have to clean it in order to start dinner. After you make yourself a snack I would like you to put away the food, put the dirty dishes in the dishwasher, and then sponge down the counters."

In the space below, combine the three parts you've already written into a complete assertive message that clarifies your expectations for your child in each of the three situations:

Situation 1: _____

_____

Situation 2: _____

_____

Situation 3: _____

_____

It's not always necessary to use all three parts of the statement, especially when a behavior has occurred more than once. If you give all the information (what you feel, why, and what you want) the first time, then a shortened version might suffice on later occasions. Emily's father might remind Emily to take his hand when they approach a street corner by the single word "Hand, Emily!" Rickie's mother might simply give him the reminder "Tell me in words," and Kai's mother might say, on entering the kitchen to prepare dinner, "Kai, the kitchen!"

Practicing Assertive Communication

Consider the following example situations and develop responses that would let the child know what you want. A sample response for each situation is given at the end of the exercise.

1. Nine-year-old Andy comes home from school with a note from the teacher saying that he didn't turn in his end-of-term project. Andy says he lost it. You spent many hours helping him with that project and making sure that it was finished by the required day.

_____

_____

_____

_____

2. Five-year-old Meg seems perfectly content to play by herself until you receive or decide to make a phone call. Like clockwork, she's at your elbow once again, asking questions or needing to talk to you.

_____

_____

_____

_____

3. One-year-old Ben loves "playing" with his four-year-old sister Hallie. He knocks over her block castles and breaks up her puz-

zles. Hallie's response is to lash out and hit Ben, which usually results in tears for Ben and a spanking for Hallie. This time you decide to try something different.

_____

_____

_____

_____

4. Eight-year-old Tommy has a hundred and one stalling tactics when it's bedtime. He's finally down for the night and you start organizing the project you brought home from work. Suddenly there he is again; he "remembered" something he needed to tell you.

_____

_____

_____

_____

Sample Responses

1. Andy, when I spend a lot of time helping you with a school project and you lose it, I feel very disappointed and unappreciated. I'd like you to take better care of your projects in general, but right now I want you to make a full search for this one.

2. (After excusing yourself from the phone conversation for a moment) Meg, when you interrupt me on the phone I get really frustrated. I can't pay attention to my friend and you at the same time. I end up not hearing either of you. I would like you to wait till I'm off the phone before talking to me, unless it's a real emergency.

3. Hallie, I'm really disappointed and angry when you hit Ben because he's just a baby and doesn't really mean to upset you. I'm also scared that you might injure him. If you're worried that Ben's going to mess up your games I want you to tell me and I'll take Ben away. If Ben gets into your stuff, I want you to tell me and I'll handle it. I don't want you to hit him.

4. Tommy, when you keep getting up like this I feel very frustrated. It means that I'm going to have to stay up later finishing this project and then be very tired tomorrow. If you remember things you need to tell me or things you have to do before school tomorrow, I want you to write a word down to remind yourself and we'll deal with them in the morning.

Choices and Consequences

Sometimes you can avoid a struggle with your children by giving them choices about something you want them to do. Offer a choice of when, how, or with whom a certain event occurs—not *whether* it occurs. If you want your daughter to have a bath, ask her whether she'd like her bath before or after a book, or whether she'd like her bath with or without bubbles, or whether she'd prefer her mom or dad to bathe her. But don't ask if she'd like a bath, if that's not really a choice. Only give choices that you're prepared to honor. Giving children choices helps them learn that they have the power to make their own decisions and that their decisions are respected by you.

In general, once you've clarified to your kids what you want and expect, they always have an implicit choice: to meet that expectation or not. When they choose not to, it's appropriate that they experience some consequences from that choice. After all, if a child does obey your request, he or she hopefully experiences some positive consequences, not least of which is your pleasure and appreciation. And just as it's important for children to learn that they have the power to make decisions, it's equally important that they learn to be responsible for the consequences that follow.

Your job is to decide what an appropriate consequence is to any particular misbehavior. There are three key issues to consider in designing consequences:

- The consequence must be related to the misbehavior.

- Once a consequence is designed, you must be willing to *follow through* with it.

- You must present the consequence calmly, without anger or blame. You're simply the neutral agent administering the consequence for whichever choice your child makes. "It seems you've chosen _____ (the consequence)" is a useful way of framing your statement.

It's important that the consequence be related to the misbehavior for your child to understand the connection between the two. Suppose your two-year-old is playing with her milk and spills it on the floor. You could send her to her room for playing with it, or you could supervise her efforts at cleaning it up. Getting sent away can feel like punishment and may elicit anger and resentment. Worse, no useful learning takes place. On the other hand, learning that when you spill something you have to clean it up facilitates the development of responsibility.

Making sure that your consequence is related to the misbehavior applies to proportion as well: a small transgression needs to be met with a similarly small consequence. When your child spills her milk, it's not useful to decree that she eat all her meals alone in the kitchen for a month. But when she draws all over your walls, it's not sufficient to simply take her markers away for an hour. When the misbehavior and consequence are out of balance there's very little opportunity for learning. The age-appropriateness of your expectations for your child's behavior, and the age-appropriateness of the consequence are also important. Remember that a two-year-old won't clean up the milk as well as a five-year-old will.

When you warn the child about the consequence of a particular choice, it's extremely important that you follow through with it. Don't threaten to cancel the whole birthday party if you have no intention of doing that. Don't tell your child that you won't go camping if you really want to go. If you don't follow through on your stated consequence, you are teaching your child that you don't mean what you say. You are teaching him or her not to trust you.

The importance of presenting the consequence without anger or blame can't be overstated. As explained earlier, anger is inherently punishing to your child and will interfere with his or her ability to learn to take responsibility for choices. It can be useful to see yourself simply as the neutral person who's carrying out the consequence linked to the choice your child made. Your child had a choice, made it, and here are the consequences.

Practicing Choices and Consequences

It's best to anticipate your child's most common misbehaviors and offer the choices and related consequences beforehand. Once you've clarified what behavior you want, it's appropriate to state the consequences of choosing to follow your request and not following it. For example, remember Emily, whose father was terrified when she pulled away from him while crossing the street? After telling her that he wanted her to hold his hand all the way across, Emily's father might say, "We can walk together if you hold my hand; if you don't I'll have to pick you up and carry you when we cross the street."

Remember Rickie, who had the tantrum in the store because his mother wouldn't buy him candy? After telling him that she wanted him to express his disappointment in words, Rickie's mother might have decided to add a consequence for noncompliance. In the space below, write an example of the appropriate choices and related consequences that she might have offered Rickie.

Choices and consequences: _____

_____

_____

_____

Sample answer: Rickie's mother might have said, "If you decide to have a tantrum, I'll take you right home and do my shopping alone next time. If you get frustrated and tell me in words, I'm glad to take you shopping with me."

Remember Kai, who left such a mess in the kitchen? After telling him what she wanted, Kai's mother might also have presented choices and consequences. In the space below, write an example of the choices and related consequences she might have offered.

Choices and consequences: _____

_____

_____

_____

Sample answer: Kai's mother might have said, "If you leave the kitchen in a mess, I won't be able to cook your dinner. You'll have to fend for yourself."

In the spaces below, list your child's three most common misbehaviors. Next to each misbehavior, write an appropriate choice and related consequence, as if you were speaking directly to your child.

Misbehavior 1: _____

Choices and consequences: _____

_____

_____

Misbehavior 2: _____

Choices and consequences: _____

_____

_____

Misbehavior 3: _____

Choices and consequences: _____

_____

_____

Time-Out—A Special Consequence

Time-out means just that: time away from whatever is going on. Usually this means that your child will go to his or her room for a specified amount of time (a few minutes for a young child is enough). This is not punishment—the child can go to his or her bedroom and play with toys—it's a time to reflect. If children choose to behave inappropriately around other people, then they need time away from everybody. Attention is a powerful reward, so time away from attention has a lot of impact on a child. Some people use the bathroom as the time-out room, because it's boring and the child is therefore less likely to get distracted from thinking about his or her misbehavior. Whichever you use, remember that for a very young child, you need to ensure that the room is safe to be alone in.

Time-outs work best when used as a consequence for misbehavior around other people. This makes sense in terms of relating consequences to the misbehavior. If your child refuses to put away his toys before bed, it makes sense to tell him "If we have to waste time waiting for you to put away your toys, there won't be time for a story," or "If you don't take care of your toys by putting them away after you use them, then I guess you won't be able to play with them tomorrow." It makes less sense to say, "If you don't put away your toys, you'll have to have a time-out," because the consequence of time away from others is not really related to the misbehavior of failing to put away toys.

It's essential that you remain calm, with your voice free of anger and blame, when sending your child to time-out. As soon as you lose your cool, you've lost control of the situation. Remind yourself that you're simply helping your child learn to take responsibility for his or her behavior.

Use a clock timer, placed out of reach, to let a child know when the time-out is over. By letting the ring of the bell signal that it's time to come out, you can give up the role of jailer. For very young children (two or younger), don't even set the timer. Simply tell little children that they can come out when they decide they want to behave better, when they want to stop hitting, pinching, biting, or whatever.

It's important to explain time-outs to your child before you use them. Say, for example, "If you can't behave appropriately around other people, then you'll have to have a time-out away from others." Some behaviors can be easily and immediately identified as things that will lead to a time-out: hitting, kicking, spitting, biting, speaking disrespectfully, screaming. Other misbehaviors may have to be identified along the way, for example, making too much noise in company. Explain that your child can either serve his or her time-out promptly and responsibly or have extra minutes added. If he or she comes out early, the time-out will start over again.

Once the concept is explained, time-outs can be used without having to warn or threaten. It's OK to remind young children of the rule in question. You can say, for example, "People aren't for hitting" if your son looks like he's going to punch someone. Then if he chooses to hit, he earns a time-out. With an older child, whose impulse control is better developed, it isn't usually necessary to give reminders.

It's essential to be consistent with the use of time-outs. If hitting another child is a behavior deserving of time-out, then every time your child hits another child, he or she needs to get a time-out. If your daughter is making too much noise while you're trying to talk to guests, you may tell her to quiet down or she'll have to go to her room for a time-out. If she chooses to continue the ruckus, follow through with the time-out. Don't continue to give warnings or threats—you don't want to teach your child that you don't mean what you say.

Special Situations

When you first introduce time-outs, your child will probably resist it. If he or she won't go willingly, give the choice of walking to the bedroom, or being carried. If the child continues to resist, say calmly, "I see you've chosen to be carried" and then carry him or her to the room and put him or her down gently. (Remember, this is not punishment. Administer the consequence without anger.) Remind the child that the timer will ring when he or she can come out. If the child yells at you or otherwise misbehaves while resisting, calmly add another minute to the time-out.

If your child won't stay in the room for the time-out, remind him or her that coming out of the room before the time is up means starting the time-out over again. If the child comes out anyway, don't get caught in a game of carrying him or her back to the room a dozen times. Simply remind the child that until the entire time-out is served, he or she may not participate in any activity outside of the bedroom.

If your child seems out of control, screaming and yelling, kicking the door, or throwing toys in the bedroom, remind him or her that "The time-out will begin only when things quiet down. Time-out is for reflection." Then simply let your child experience the consequences of his or her actions. If your daughter breaks a toy, she'll have a broken toy. If your son pulls all the bedclothes off his bed, or makes a mess of the room, he'll have to clean it up.

When time-out is over, welcome your child back without anger. Even a few minutes away can seem like a very long time to a child.

Problem-Solving Communication

When a problem has recurred, and clarifying what you want hasn't worked, you might try engaging your child in problem solving. Your child may have some surprising insights into why he or she misbehaves, as well as some ideas about what could be done about it. To find out, however, you have to be willing to sit down and listen respectfully to what your child has to say. There are six steps to problem solving:

1. *Talk about your child's feelings and needs.* This is important. Don't assume you know. Ask for clarification: "I'm not sure I understand why that's a problem for you," or "Tell me exactly what you want here," or "How do you actually feel about that?" If your child doesn't believe you're really interested in understanding his or her feelings and needs, or thinks that you're only giving lip service to the "joint" aspect of problem solving, then you'll be wasting your time. Also, sometimes the problem you're focused on isn't the real problem; by exploring your child's feelings and needs you may be able to open a curtain on the underlying difficulty.

2. *Talk about your own feelings and needs.* Keep this succinct. The idea is not to try to convince your child that your needs or feelings are more important or weighty. The concept you want to convey is that both of you have feelings and needs and that both of your feelings and needs are valid.

3. *Brainstorm all possible solutions without judgment.* If possible, let the child come up with the first couple of suggestions. Encourage lighthearted alternatives as well as more serious ones, and write down everything, without analyzing.

4. *Eliminate those solutions that are not mutually agreeable.* Go back over your list and cross off solutions that *either* of you finds unacceptable. If you think one wouldn't work, say so without criticism. Don't use statements such as "That's a stupid suggestion." You can also take this opportunity to explain why you think an alternative *would* work. If at the end of this step you find yourselves without anything left on your list, you have two options: You can reconsider some of the solutions you crossed off your list, or you can brainstorm more alternatives.

5. *Pick the best solution (or combination of alternatives).* You need to have at least one mutually agreeable solution remaining on your list before you can proceed to this step. If

there are a variety of options left on the list, decide together which one you want to try.

6. *Develop a plan for implementation and evaluation.* Decide how long you want to try the new plan before evaluating its success. It's also best to develop a fallback plan in case the first solution doesn't work. Sometimes a fallback plan will be one of the other alternatives on your list (the second best choice). At other times the fallback plan might involve consequences designed by either you alone or in consultation with your child.

Nine-year-old Mike had been forgetting to feed his dog on a regular basis. His mother had expressed her expectations very clearly: "Mike, when I see your dog staring hungrily at her empty bowl, I get upset that she's not being taken care of properly. You need to remember to feed her every morning." Mike always responded to those reminders with a quick apology and by putting out the food. But the problem didn't change. So Mike's mother decided to try a new approach: joint problem solving. One evening she asked Mike to talk with her for a while and he agreed.

Step 1: Talk about your child's feelings and needs.

Mother: Mike, I've seen Goldie miss her regular feeding time four times this week. I know you love her and want her to get the care she needs. Do you see this as a problem?

Mike: Not really—she always gets fed sooner or later.

Mother: So your feeling is that as long as she eventually gets fed it's OK?

Mike: Well . . . I guess.

Step 2: Talk about your own feelings and needs.

Mother: Well, I feel badly for Goldie. Often she gets fed only because I remind you, and sometimes she's waited hours past her usual feeding time. I don't like to think of her being hungry and miserable. And it worries me that if I didn't remind you, she might not get fed at all.

Step 3: Brainstorm all possible solutions, without judgment.

Mother: What can we do about it? Let's brainstorm. I'll write our suggestions down. Let's not decide if they're any good, let's just list them.

Mike: (teasing) Well, you could feed her for me!

Mother: (writing it down) That's one idea. I have one, too— that we find Goldie a home where she'll be better cared for.

Mike: No! How about if I get her a huge bucket and fill it with food and let her eat out of it all week.

Mother: Or we could have a memory aid: If you forget to feed her in the morning, you won't watch TV or do any other fun thing that you've planned when you get home from school that day.

Mike: Nice, Mom. Maybe I could feed her in the afternoon instead of in the morning? I'd be less rushed then, and I could take her for a walk, too.

Step 4: Eliminate those alternative solutions that are not mutually agreeable.

Mother: If neither of us has any more suggestions, let's go through our list and evaluate. I'll read out each suggestion, and if either of us doesn't want it, then I'll cross it out. The first one is, I could feed Goldie for you. I'm not willing to keep that as an alternative. She's not my dog, so I don't want that responsibility. (crosses it off the list) The next one is, we find Goldie a home where she'll be better cared for.

Mike: No! Forget about that!

Mother: OK. You could fill a big bucket with food and let her eat out of it all week. I don't think you'd like it if I left a big bowl of oatmeal on the table for you to eat out of all week.

Mike: Yuck! OK, cross that off.

Mother: If you forget to feed her in the morning, you don't watch TV or do any other fun thing that's planned for that day.

Mike: I'm sure that's the one you like. But I like my next suggestion better.

Mother: That you feed her in the afternoon when you get home from school? That would be OK with me, too. So we have two possible solutions.

Step 5: Pick the best solution (or combination of alternatives).

Mother: Which would work best?

Mike: I want to try feeding her in the afternoon when I get home from school.

Step 6: Develop a plan for implementation and evaluation.

Mother: OK. That sounds good to me. When do we start, and when should we evaluate how it's working?

Mike: Tomorrow. If I haven't fed her by the time you get home, I won't watch TV (fallback plan). Let's try it for a week and see how it's working then.

Mother: Great. I'm really glad you were willing to solve this problem with me. I know how much you love

Goldie. (Notice that Mom reinforces the problem solving behavior that she'd like to see again.)

Effective parenting is rooted in respect for your child. Any attempt at problem solving that communicates respect for your child's feelings, needs, and ideas, will enhance your relationship while reducing misbehavior.

8

Your Master Plan for Anger Control

This chapter provides a framework for controlling your anger in situations you find especially provocative. In this chapter you'll bring together techniques from the previous chapters, combining them in a master plan to follow the next time you're faced with a recurring problem situation.

Example Master Plan

Sally's six-year-old daughter, Gina, was a "bear" in the mornings. She dragged herself out of bed, plopped in front of the TV, wouldn't eat breakfast, was chronically late for school, and inspired huge screaming matches with her mom at least once a week.

Sally needed a master plan for dealing with anger in the mornings. She wasn't a morning person herself, so she needed a clear plan that she could follow automatically, without having to make anything up on the spot. Here is the master plan she formulated.

Anger Control Master Plan

Problem Situation: *Gina gets up late, won't eat or dress, late for school, throws tantrum if pressured to get ready on time.*

Changing What You Think

Trigger thoughts: *She's lazy, mean, contrary. I can't stand this. It's unfair. She's defying me.*
Alternative explanation for child's behavior:
    Temperament *She's highly reactive to every transition.*
    Developmental stage *She craves freedom and autonomy.*
    Underlying needs *Needs food—low blood sugar.*
    Reinforcement   .

Talking back to trigger thoughts: *She has a hard time waking up. And she needs food. It's nothing personal. I can cope and plan around her.*

Changing What You Do

Notice early warning signs: *Feel warm, nervous stomach, headache.*
Brief coping assertions: *Stay calm. You can cope.*
Cue yourself to relax: *"Breathe in . . . Relax."*
Plan to provide for child's real need: *Hand her orange juice without comment, get blood sugar up before asking her to do anything.*

Changing What You Say

Assertive statement:
    When you *aren't dressed by 7:30 and fed by 8:00* I feel *frustrated and worried because your teacher gets irritated when we're late, and I end up late for work and I want you to stick to the schedule: dressing by 7:30 and cereal by 8:00.*
Offer choices: *Dress yourself or I'll choose and you'll dress in the car. Eat what I fix or have a bagel in the car.*
Describe consequences: *We leave for school at 8:15, whether you have the clothes and breakfast and homework you want or not.*
Time-out? ___ Yes _X_ No
Problem-solving conversation? _X_ Yes When? *In the evening.*
                                        ____ No
Possible alternative solutions: *Eat bagels in car every morning. Sleep in clean underwear. No TV in mornings.*

Sally finished her plan on the weekend. On Monday morning she woke Gina and went downstairs to make coffee and pour orange juice. She handed Gina a glass of orange juice silently. Gina growled at her, but Sally still said nothing out loud. She repeated one of her coping statements to herself: "Don't take it personally, she has a hard time with every transition."

After Gina had finished the orange juice, Sally asked her to get dressed. Gina just frowned at her and continued to watch television. Sally started to feel warm, with a nervous sensation in her stomach—the warning signs that she was getting angry. She gave herself the relaxation cues she'd been practicing: "Breathe in . . . Relax."

Her anger subsided enough for her to say to Gina in a neutral tone, "You can pick out your own clothes to wear today and put them on by 7:30. If you're not dressed by then, I'll pick something for you myself."

She turned off the television and walked into the kitchen to fix breakfast. At 7:30 she checked on Gina, who was mostly dressed but still barefoot. Sally tried her assertive statement:

"When you aren't dressed by 7:30, I feel frustrated and worried, because your teacher gets irritated when we're late, and I end up late for work. Get your shoes on and come eat your oatmeal."

Sally left the room, telling herself, "Don't take it personally. It's just the way she is. All kids do this sort of thing."

At 8:15 Gina had her socks on and had taken one or two bites of oatmeal. Sally said, "I see you've decided to let me pick the shoes and to eat in the car. Let's go, it's time to leave."

Gina was rather stunned as Sally hustled her into the car with her red shoes and a bagel hastily spread with peanut butter. Gina complained, but stopped well short of her usual tantrum level.

By the end of two weeks, Sally's master plan had become a matter of habit. No further problem solving was necessary. It worked so well because she planned in advance what she would think, what she would do, and what she would say.

Sally paid attention to her early warning signs, and used her coping self-statements before her trigger thoughts could catapult her into an angry outburst.

She didn't respond to provocation. Instead, she paused and took a couple of deep breaths. During that pause, she reviewed her coping statements and reminded herself of what Gina really needed from her.

Sally provided what Gina really needed in the morning: undisturbed time to wake up in front of TV, orange juice to raise her blood sugar and make her less irritable, freedom to choose her wardrobe, minimal hassles and distractions, clear choices and logical consequences, and a regular, nonnegotiable departure time for school.

Creating Your Own Master Plan

Use the following form to draft your master plan. You probably won't fill in every blank for every problem situation, but using the form will remind you of all your anger control options, and you can choose the ones that apply to a given situation.

Problem Situation: _____

_____

_____

Changing What You Think (from chapters 3, 4, and 5)

Trigger thoughts: _____

_____

Alternative explanations for child's behavior:

    Temperament _____

    Developmental stage _____

    Underlying needs _____

    Reinforcement _____

    Talking back to trigger thoughts (page 96): _____

_____

_____

_____

Changing What You Do (from chapter 6)

    Notice early warning signs: _____

    Brief coping thoughts: _____

    Cue yourself to relax: "Breathe in . . . Relax." _____

    Plan to provide for child's real need: _____

Changing What You Say (from chapter 7)

    Assertive statement:

        When you _____

        I feel _____

        because _____

        and I want _____

    Offer choices (pages 129-131): _____

    Describe consequences: _____

    Time-out? ____ Yes ____ No

    Problem-solving conversation? ____ Yes When? _____
                                   ____ No

    Possible alternative solutions: _____

    _____

    _____

A

Parental Anger Survey
Methodology and Results

The Parental Anger Survey generated 250 completed question-naires in response to ads in national parenting magazines. Ninety-two percent of the respondents were mothers.

Three measures were used to assess anger levels: (1) the Parental Anger Inventory (DeRoma and Hansen 1994), (2) a ten-point Likert scale rating of "How often do you find yourself angry at your child?" and (3) a ten-point Likert scale rating of "When you are angry at your child, on average how angry do you get?"

t-tests were performed to compare mean frequency scores of twenty-four trigger thoughts and twenty-four coping thoughts or behaviors for high- versus low-anger parents (using the three measures described above). Trigger thoughts significantly related to anger scores (those that parents with *high* anger levels reported experiencing significantly more often) are presented in Table 1. Coping thoughts significantly related to anger scores (those that parents with *low* anger levels reported experiencing significantly more often) are presented in Table 2. Coping behaviors significantly related to anger scores (those that parents with *low* anger levels reported experiencing significantly more often) are reported in Table 3.

Table 1
Trigger Thoughts Significantly Related to Anger Scores

Trigger Thought	t-test with PAI	t-test with Anger Amplitude	t-test with Anger Frequency
You're doing it to annoy me.	t=3.12 p=0.00	t=4.30 p=0.00	t=3.71 p=0.00
You're defying me.	t=3.60 p=0.00	t=5.54 p=0.00	t=4.60 p=0.00
You're trying to drive me crazy.	t=3.13 p=0.00	t=3.87 p=0.00	t=5.05 p=0.00
You're trying to test me (see how far you can go).	t=4.17 p=0.00	t=3.95 p=0.00	t=5.29 p=0.00
You're tuning me out intentionally.	t=3.15 p=0.00	t=3.78 p=0.00	t=3.57 p=0.00
You're taking advantage of me.	t=3.42 p=0.00	t=4.02 p=0.00	t=2.46 p=0.01
You're doing this deliberately (to get back at me, hurt me, spite me, etc.).	t=3.73 p=0.00	t=4.43 p=0.00	t=3.11 p=0.00
I can't stand it.	t=4.04 p=0.00	t=6.39 p=0.00	t=3.83 p=0.00
This behavior is intolerable.	t=4.00 p=0.00	t=4.89 p=0.00	t=3.40 p=0.00
You've gone too far this time.	t=3.48 p=0.00	t=4.51 p=0.00	t=3.69 p=0.00
You never listen.	t=3.92 p=0.00	t=4.38 p=0.00	t=5.79 p=0.00

How dare you (look at me like that, talk to me like that, do that, etc.).	t=4.91 p=0.00	t=5.49 p=0.00	t=5.01 p=0.00
You turn everything into a (power struggle, fight, lousy time together, nightmare, etc.).	t=3.08 p=0.00	t=4.20 p=0.00	t=3.25 p=0.00
You're getting out of control.	t=3.22 p=0.00	t=5.04 p=0.00	t=3.29 p=0.00
This is manipulation.	t=3.45 p=0.00	t=2.66 p=0.00	t=1.69 p=ns
You're so (lazy, malicious, stubborn, disrespectful, ungrateful, willful, selfish, cruel, stupid, bratty, spoiled, contrary, etc.).	t=3.23 p=0.00	t=4.48 p=0.00	t=3.84 p=0.00
You're deliberately being mean, a jerk, etc.	t=3.72 p=0.00	t=5.08 p=0.00	t=4.44 p=0.00
You don't care (what happens, how I feel, who you hurt, etc.).	t=3.75 p=0.00	t=4.29 p=0.00	t=2.88 p=0.00

Table 2
Coping Thoughts Significantly Related to Anger Scores

Coping Thought	*t-test with PAI*	*t-test with Anger Amplitude*	*t-test with Anger Frequency*
It's just a stage, kids have to go through these stages.	t=−2.43 p=0.01	t=−1.24 p=ns	t=−0.70 p=ns
This is natural for his or her age.	t=−2.84 p=0.00	t=−1.64 p=ns	t=−2.46 p=0.01

Don't take it seriously; keep a sense of humor.	t=−2.73 p=0.00	t=−1.26 p=ns	t=−2.80 p=0.01
This is just natural impulsiveness.	t=−1.04 p=ns	t=−2.46 p=0.01	t=−0.94 p=ns
He or she isn't really trying to do it to me, it's just how he or she is coping right now.	t=−2.30 p=0.05	t=−2.61 p=0.01	t=−3.06 p=0.00
He or she can't help (crying, being angry, interrupting, needing attention, etc.).	t=−3.27 p=0.00	t=−1.09 p=ns	t=−0.98 p=ns
Just get through it. You can cope. You don't have to get angry.	t=−1.09 p=ns	t=−0.80 p=ns	t=−2.21 p=0.05

Table 3
Coping Behaviors Significantly Related to Anger Scores

Coping Behavior	*t-test with PAI*	*t-test with Anger Amplitude*	*t-test with Anger Frequency*
Taking a deep breath, telling myself to relax before saying anything.	t=−1.06 p=ns	t=−1.37 p=ns	t=−2.47 p=0.01
Trying to give the child what he or she really needs: attention, praise, physical affection, solving a problem.	t=−2.70 p=0.00	t=−1.27 p=ns	t=−1.78 p=ns

B

Questionnaires Used in the Parental Anger Survey

Anger Questionnaire I

Circle the number that best describes how often these thoughts occur.

When I'm angry at my kids I tend to say to myself:

	Never		Rarely		Sometimes		Often		Always
1. You're doing it to annoy me.	1	2	3	4	5	6	7	8	9
2. You know better (but you're not choosing to do it).	1	2	3	4	5	6	7	8	9
3. I can't stand it.	1	2	3	4	5	6	7	8	9
4. You don't care (what happens, how I feel, who you hurt, etc.).	1	2	3	4	5	6	7	8	9
5. You're defying me.	1	2	3	4	5	6	7	8	9

	Never	*Rarely*	*Sometimes*	*Often*	*Always*
6. You're getting out of control.	1 2 3	4 5 6	7 8 9		
7. This behavior is intolerable.	1 2 3	4 5 6	7 8 9		
8. You're trying to drive me crazy.	1 2 3	4 5 6	7 8 9		
9. You're doing this deliberately (to get back at me, hurt me, spite me, etc.).	1 2 3	4 5 6	7 8 9		
10. You really deserve to be punished.	1 2 3	4 5 6	7 8 9		
11. You've gone too far this time.	1 2 3	4 5 6	7 8 9		
12. You're trying to test me (see how far you can go).	1 2 3	4 5 6	7 8 9		
13. You're trying to control me.	1 2 3	4 5 6	7 8 9		
14. This is manipulation.	1 2 3	4 5 6	7 8 9		
15. You're trying to keep me from (getting rest, having fun, getting my work done, etc.).	1 2 3	4 5 6	7 8 9		
16. You're so (lazy, malicious, stubborn, disrespectful, ungrateful, willful, selfish, cruel, stupid, bratty, spoiled, contrary, etc.).	1 2 3	4 5 6	7 8 9		
17. You're deliberately being mean, a jerk, etc.	1 2 3	4 5 6	7 8 9		
18. You're trying to get away with _____.	1 2 3	4 5 6	7 8 9		
19. You never listen.	1 2 3	4 5 6	7 8 9		

	Never	Rarely	Sometimes	Often	Always

20. How dare you (look at me like that, talk to me like that, do that, etc.). 1 2 3 4 5 6 7 8 9

21. You're tuning me out intentionally. 1 2 3 4 5 6 7 8 9

22. You're taking advantage of me. 1 2 3 4 5 6 7 8 9

23. I didn't get _____, why should you? 1 2 3 4 5 6 7 8 9

24. You turn everything into a (power struggle, fight, lousy time together, nightmare, etc.). 1 2 3 4 5 6 7 8 9

Anger Questionnaire II

Circle the number that best describes how often these thoughts or responses occur.

When I'm angry at my kids I tend to cope by:

	Never	Rarely	Sometimes	Often	Always

1. Thinking "It's just a stage; kids have to go through these stages." 1 2 3 4 5 6 7 8 9

2. Thinking "They're just kids." Or thinking "Kids will be kids." 1 2 3 4 5 6 7 8 9

3. Removing myself from the situation and going back later. 1 2 3 4 5 6 7 8 9

4. Focusing on other things, distracting myself. 1 2 3 4 5 6 7 8 9

	Never		Rarely		Sometimes		Often		Always
5. Isolating the child for a little while, using "time-out."	1	2	3	4	5	6	7	8	9
6. Trying to give the child what he or she *really* needs: attention, praise, physical affection, solving a problem, etc.	1	2	3	4	5	6	7	8	9
7. Thinking "He or she just needs more attention, help, praise."	1	2	3	4	5	6	7	8	9
8. Reminding myself "Just be consistent, draw the limits always in the same place. I need to show him or her where the line is."	1	2	3	4	5	6	7	8	9
9. Taking a deep breath, telling myself to relax before saying anything.	1	2	3	4	5	6	7	8	9
10. Thinking "Don't take it seriously; keep a sense of humor."	1	2	3	4	5	6	7	8	9
11. Thinking "It's not his or her fault: my child's doing the best he or she can in the situation."	1	2	3	4	5	6	7	8	9
12. Thinking "Kids make mistakes." Or thinking "No kid is perfect."	1	2	3	4	5	6	7	8	9
13. Thinking "This is just natural impulsiveness."	1	2	3	4	5	6	7	8	9

	Never	Rarely	Sometimes	Often	Always
14. Thinking "This is natural for his or her age."	1　2	3　4	5　6	7　8	9
15. Removing the child from the situation. For example, leaving a store.	1　2	3　4	5　6	7　8	9
16. Thinking "I don't want to hurt my child; this is *my* child."	1　2	3　4	5　6	7　8	9
17. Looking for the other sources of my anger, not just my child."	1　2	3　4	5　6	7　8	9
18. Thinking "Frustration with kids is normal, expected."	1　2	3　4	5　6	7　8	9
19. Thinking "Pushing limits is normal" or "Tantrums are normal."	1　2	3　4	5　6	7　8	9
20. Thinking "He or she can't help (crying, being angry, interrupting, needing attention)."	1　2	3　4	5　6	7　8	9
21. Remembering that he or she isn't really trying to do it to me; it's just how he or she is coping right now.	1　2	3　4	5　6	7　8	9
22. Trying to remember how much I love him or her.	1　2	3　4	5　6	7　8	9
23. Thinking "Just get through it. You can cope. You don't have to get angry."	1　2	3　4	5　6	7　8	9
24. Thinking up reasonable consequences if my child doesn't do what I ask.	1　2	3　4	5　6	7　8	9

Anger Questionnaire III

1. How often do you find yourself angry at your child (children)?

    Never   Rarely   Sometimes   Often   Always

    1   2   3   4   5   6   7   8   9   10

2. When you are angry at your child (children), on average how angry do you get?

    Slightly   Somewhat   Moderately   Very   Enraged
    Irritated   Angry   Angry   Angry

    1   2   3   4   5   6   7   8   9   10

3. On average, I shout or scream at my child (children):

    _____ times per week;

or, if less than once a week, _____ times per month;

or, if less than once a month, _____ times per year.

Statistical Information

Your age _____ Sex _____

Mark one: _____ Single-parent family

    _____ Two-parent family

    _____ Shared custody

Number of children _____

Ages of children _____

Mark one: _____ Rural environment

_____ Suburban environment

_____ Urban environment

Mark one: _____ Didn't graduate high school

_____ High school graduate

_____ Some college

_____ College graduate

_____ Graduate work

Number of hours worked per week _____

Number of hours spent with children per week _____

Mark one: _____ Born in the United States

_____ Grew up in another culture (please specify)

_____

Family income: _____ Less than $30,000

_____ $30,000 to $60,000

_____ $60,000 to $90,000

_____ over $90,000

References

Ames, Louise Bates, and Carol Chase Haber. 1976. *Your Seven-Year-Old*. New York: Dell Publishing.

———. 1989. *Your Eight-Year-Old*. New York: Dell Publishing.

———. 1990. *Your Nine-Year-Old*. New York: Dell Publishing.

Ames, Louise Bates, and Frances L. Ilg. 1976. *Your Two-Year-Old*. New York: Dell Publishing.

———. 1976. *Your Four-Year-Old*. New York: Dell Publishing.

———. 1979a. *Your Five-Year-Old*. New York: Dell Publishing.

———. 1979b. *Your Six-Year-Old*. New York: Dell Publishing.

———. 1985. *Your Three-Year-Old*. New York: Dell Publishing.

Ames, Louise B., Frances L. Ilg, and Carol Chase Haber. 1982. *Your One-Year-Old*. New York: Dell Publishing.

Crockenberg, Susan. 1985. "Toddlers' Reactions to Maternal Anger." *Merril-Palmer Quarterly* 31:361–373.

————. 1987. "Predictors and Correlates of Anger Toward and Punitive Control of Toddlers by Adolescent Mothers." *Child Development* 58:964–975.

Davis, M., E. R. Eshelman, and M. McKay. 1994. *The Relaxation & Stress Reduction Workbook,* 4th ed. Oakland, Calif.: New Harbinger Publications.

DeRoma, V. M., and D. J. Hansen. 1994. Development of the Parental Anger Inventory. Presented at the Association for the Advancement of Behavior Therapy Convention, San Diego, Calif., November.

Dinkmeyer, D., and G.D. McKay, 1983. *The Parent's Guide: Systematic Training for Effective Parenting of Teens.* Circle Pines, Minnesota: American Guidance Service.

Dreikurs, Rudolf, M.D., with Vicki Soltz, R.N. 1964. *Children: The Challenge.* New York: Hawthorn Books.

Frude, N., and A. Goss. 1979."Parental Anger: A General Population Survey." *Child Abuse and Neglect* 3:331–333.

Grevin, Phillip. 1990. *Spare the Child: The Religious Roots of Punishment and the Psychological Impact of Physical Abuse.* New York: Knopf.

Hemenway, David, Sara Solnick, and Jennifer Carter. 1994. "Child Rearing Violence." *Child Abuse and Neglect* 18: 1011–1020.

Heusson, Carol. 1986. *Parental Anger: An Examination of Cognitive and Situational Factors.* Dissertation. University of Waterloo, Ontario, Canada.

Korbanka, Juergen, and Matthew McKay. 1995. "The Emotional and Behavioral Effects of Parental Discipline Styles on Their Adult Children." Unpublished paper.

McKay, Matthew, Peter D. Rogers, and Judith McKay. 1989. *When Anger Hurts.* Oakland, Calif.: New Harbinger Publications.

Oliver, J. 1993. "Intergenerational Transmission of Child Abuse: Rates, Research, and Clinical Implications." *American Journal of Psychiatry* 150:1315–1324.

San Francisco Examiner. Dec. 7, 1995. "Child Abuse Figures Soar in U.S. Poll."

Strassberg, Zvi, Kenneth Dodge, Gregory Pettit, and John Bates. 1994. "Spanking in the Home and Children's Subsequent Aggression Toward Kindergarten Peers." *Development and Psychology* Vol 6, No 3: 445–461.

Straus, Murray. 1994. *Beating the Devil Out of Them: Corporal Punishment in American Families.* New York: Lexington Books.

Tesser, Abraham, Rex Forehand, Gene Brody, and Nicholas Long. 1989. "Conflict: The Role of Calm and Angry Parent-Child Discussion in Adolescent Adjustment." *Journal of Social and Clinical Psychology* 8:317–330.

Trickett, Penelope, and Leon Kuczynski. 1986. "Children's Misbehaviors and Parental Discipline Strategies in Abusive and Non-Abusive Families." *Developmental Psychology* 22:115–123.

Turecki, Stanley, with Leslie Tonner. 1985. *The Difficult Child.* New York: Bantam Books.

Zaidi, Lisa, John Knutson, and John Mehm. 1989. "Transgenerational Patterns of Abusive Parenting." *Aggressive Behavior* 15:137–152.

Matthew McKay, Ph.D., is a founding director of Haight Ashbury Psychological Services and co-director of Brief Therapy Associates in San Francisco. Dr. McKay is co-author of eleven books, including *Self-Esteem, The Relaxation & Stress Reduction Workbook, When Anger Hurts,* and *Couple Skills.* In private practice he specializes in the treatment of anxiety, anger, and depression. Dr. McKay is on the faculty of the Wright Institute in Berkeley.

Patrick Fanning is a professional writer in the mental health field and the founder of a men's support group in northern California. He has co-authored seven self-help books including *Thoughts & Feelings, Messages: The Communication Skills Book, Self-Esteem, Being a Man, Prisoners of Belief,* and *The Addiction Workbook.* He has also authored *Visualization for Change* and *Lifetime Weight Control.*

Kim Paleg, Ph.D., is a clinical psychologist in private practice in San Francisco and El Sobrante, California. Dr. Paleg is co-author of *Couple Skills,* and a contributing author to the self-help classic *When Anger Hurts.* She also co-edited a widely used professional text, *Focal Group Psychotherapy.* Her book, *Ten Things Every Parent Needs to Know,* is forthcoming. She specializes in couples and family therapy and conducts workshops on parenting.

Dana Landis worked as a counselor at a battered women's shelter in Santa Cruz, California, and for two years was the research coordinator for the parental anger study on which this book is based. As part of the pilot study, she conducted in-depth interviews with parents who explored their experiences with anger. A contributing writer to the forthcoming second edition of *Thoughts & Feelings,* Ms. Landis is currently in a Ph.D. program in psychology at DePaul University.

Some Other
New Harbinger Titles

Helping Your Depressed Child, Item 3228 $14.95

The Couples's Guide to Love and Money, Item 3112 $18.95

50 Wonderful Ways to be a Single-Parent Family, Item 3082 $12.95

Caring for Your Grieving Child, Item 3066 $14.95

Helping Your Child Overcome an Eating Disorder, Item 3104 $16.95

Helping Your Angry Child, Item 3120 $17.95

The Stepparent's Survival Guide, Item 3058 $17.95

Drugs and Your Kid, Item 3015 $15.95

The Daughter-In-Law's Survival Guide, Item 2817 $12.95

Whose Life Is It Anyway?, Item 2892 $14.95

It Happened to Me, Item 2795 $17.95

Act it Out, Item 2906 $19.95

Parenting Your Older Adopted Child, Item 2841 $16.95

Boy Talk, Item 271X $14.95

Talking to Alzheimer's, Item 2701 $12.95

Helping a Child with Nonverbal Learning Disorder or Asperger's Syndrome, Item 2779 $14.95

The 50 Best Ways to Simplify Your Life, Item 2558 $11.95

When Anger Hurts Your Relationship, Item 2604 $13.95

The Couple's Survival Workbook, Item 254X $18.95

Loving Your Teenage Daughter, Item 2620 $14.95

The Hidden Feeling of Motherhood, Item 2485 $14.95

Parenting Well When You're Depressed, Item 2515 $17.95

Thinking Pregnant, Item 2302 $13.95

Call **toll free, 1-800-748-6273,** or log on to our online bookstore at **www.newharbinger.com** to order. Have your Visa or Mastercard number ready. Or send a check for the titles you want to New Harbinger Publications, Inc., 5674 Shattuck Ave., Oakland, CA 94609. Include $4.50 for the first book and 75¢ for each additional book, to cover shipping and handling. (California residents please include appropriate sales tax.) Allow two to five weeks for delivery.

Prices subject to change without notice.